Logan,
Thanks for a great ... good teammate for everyone.
May God Bless You!
           Coach "T"

1 Corinthians 16:13
Be on the Alert, stand firm in the faith, Act like men, be strong

"Friendship"

God, Life and Basketball

Rusty Shepperd

AuthorHouse™
1663 Liberty Drive, Suite 200
Bloomington, IN 47403
www.authorhouse.com
Phone: 1-800-839-8640

© 2008 Rusty Shepperd. All rights reserved.

No part of this book may be reproduced, stored in a retrieval system, or transmitted by any means without the written permission of the author.

First published by AuthorHouse 4/17/2008

ISBN: 978-1-4343-7008-2 (sc)

Printed in the United States of America
Bloomington, Indiana

This book is printed on acid-free paper.

Chapter I

The Beginning

Chad Palmer wasn't your typical 17 year old boy. By the time he was a Junior in high school, he had already been offered a scholarship to play basketball from every major college basketball program in the Country, he was featured on the covers of magazines, and on all of the sport networks as well. Chad was living a life that precious few others had ever dreamed about. Not only was he a standout athlete, he was tall, standing at six feet five inches, strikingly attractive, an honor student, and dating the prettiest girl in school. Every boy wanted to be him, and every girl wanted to date him. Chad thought everything in his life was complete, but one day, a friends' invitation to attend church camp changed his life forever. Chad's friend Jordan, was a year ahead of him in school, and had been a close friend since grade school. Jordan had invited Chad to church many times, but he always came up with some excuse not to go. He was either too tired, or he was doing something with his girlfriend Katherine, or he just didn't feel like going. Chad never thought much about God, church, or his soul. He did believe in God, but that was as far as his thoughts ever went on the subject. Chad had always promised to go with Jordan, and now this was his last chance to keep his word, because Jordan would be leaving after the summer to attend college. He was also ready to get away from his father for a week, because his father was constantly pressuring him to choose which college he was going to play basketball for after his Senior year. Chad knew at the camp that cell phones were not allowed, so he could just get away from the pressure and relax. Chad was also a little curious to see what the whole church thing was about, so to the surprise of everyone who knew him, he packed a suitcase, and headed off to camp.

Leaving town for a week also gave Chad a chance to see what it was like to be just another kid, instead of the star basketball player who was thought to be the greatest prospect to ever come out of the talent rich state of Indiana. When Chad arrived at camp, he got a major shock, although everyone was very nice to him, they treated him like he was just another kid, and not a celebrity. He wasn't asked for one autograph, which was a daily request usually, even from adults. He wasn't asked where he was going to play basketball in college. He wasn't even asked about basketball in any way at all. Something else was different at camp. People didn't give him special treatment. Chad couldn't remember the last time that someone didn't do, or give him something for free, just because he was a basketball star. Not only was he not treated differently from the other kids, but the staff treated him just like any other camper. Chad was expected to do all the same chores, and tasks as everyone else. He picked up trash around the camp, he washed trays and dishes, and cleaned up around the dorm in which he stayed.

When it came time for the first evening service, Chad went, listened, and learned. Chad's family didn't go to church unless it was Christmas or Easter, so when the camp pastor was speaking about all that Jesus went through, so that men and women could be saved, it touched his heart, and he wanted to learn more. That night, he sat and talked with his counselor and Jordan about Jesus, and asked them to tell him more. They answered every question he had to the best of their ability, and then they went to bed for the night. The next day, Chad kept thinking about the sermon that he heard the previous night and for the first time in his life, he thought about whether or not he would go to Heaven or Hell. Chad knew that he not only needed, but wanted to give his heart, and his life to Jesus Christ. After the sermon that night, when the minister gave the invitation to come forward and accept Jesus, he was the first one to get up and do so. Up to this point in his life, Chad had experienced all the best things that this life has to offer, but all of those paled in comparison to what he felt in that chapel the night he submitted his will and life to Jesus Christ. Something else happened that night. All of the pressure and anxiety he had been feeling about college and basketball had disappeared. He now had peace and joy in their place.

    Chad enjoyed the last three days of camp. He spent a lot of that time learning more about Jesus, and reading the Bible that was given to him from the camp after he got saved. He went to camp to get away, and to share a week with his friend that was leaving, but he never expected to ever become what he use to call a "Bible Thumper". Chad couldn't wait to get back home to share with his family and friends his new found faith. He wanted everyone he knew to feel what he felt, and become Christians too. What Chad didn't know was not everyone would be receptive to his faith, or his new way of living. He was also going to be tempted, and tested in his faith by those who were closest to him. Chad had only been a Christian for less than a week, but he was about to have an awakening to what it's like to be a Christian in a world that doesn't think, speak, act, or believe the ways that he now does. Not only that, but his friend Jordan wouldn't be there to help and encourage him through the times of temptation and trial. Chad would either have to stand strong alone, or give in and go back to the way he was before he left for camp.

Chapter II
Changes

Chad was bursting with excitement and anticipation on the way home, and he couldn't wait to share everything that happened with Katherine, the love of his life. He just knew that she too would gladly accept Jesus as her Lord and Savior, just as he did at camp last week.

Chad and Katherine had dated since the eighth grade. They had always been able to confide anything to one another. She was always there for him if his dad was on his back, or if he didn't play as well as he wanted to after a game. She was never anything but supportive to him and to all of his dreams. He too was extremely good to her. He remained true to her, even though he could have cheated on her with just about any girl he met. He always complimented her on how she looked, because even though she was beautiful, she didn't think so, and whenever she was upset because of family issues, he would talk to her on the phone all night if necessary, until she fell asleep. Many times they had dreamed together about how he would play basketball in college, then professionally, and how they would get married and raise a family together. All of those thoughts seemed even better now that Jesus was in the plan too. Or at least that was how Chad had envisioned things.

Chad called Katherine as soon as he walked in his house, and asked her to come right over, he wanted to see her. Katherine hadn't seen Chad in a week, and she missed him terribly. So she came right away. As soon as she arrived, she gave him a big hug and kiss. She also noticed that they were alone, and mentioned to Chad that it would be a good idea to take advantage of the opportunity they had, and go up to his bedroom. That is when everything started to go wrong. Chad asked Katherine to sit down. He had some things he needed to tell her. She agreed, because she thought maybe Chad and his father had already had a fight in the short time he had been back, or something even worse. Chad let her know that it was not anything bad, but in fact, it was the greatest thing to ever happen to him in his life. This statement led her to think that he had finally made up his mind which school he was going to play for. Chad told her it wasn't that either, but it was something even greater. That left Katherine not knowing what to think, so she just waited and listened. Chad began to tell her about church camp, and how much fun he had, and that he never knew what Jesus had gone through, or that he even loved him before last week. He told her that from now on he wasn't going to be like the old Chad, but he was now a full pledged Christian, and that he had never been happier or as content, and that he wanted her to share that experience. Katherine sat there for a second and then she started to laugh, she didn't believe him. Katherine thought he was just joking around because he had always been known for his jokes. Chad assured her that he was not teasing her, but he indeed had given his life to Christ, and that from now on he wasn't going to drink, curse, lie, and last but not least, he no longer was going to have improper relations with her. He told her that he wanted to wait until they were married before they ever slept together again. Katherine could not believe what she was hearing. Chad, the party animal, who drank more than anyone at every party, wasn't going to drink anymore, and not only that, but he wasn't going to have sex with her again until they're married! She didn't believe it, but she could tell that he was serious, so she decided to go along with it, and see how long it lasted. Katherine thought for sure she would have her old Chad back within a month at the longest.

As far as her becoming a Christian too, she said she would go with him to church once in a while, and check it out, but she wouldn't promise anything. Chad thought that was fair, and then they spent the rest of the day watching movies, and getting caught up on everything she did over the week they were apart.

That night when Katherine went home, she called Chad and told him that she forgot to mention that his best friend from the basketball team, Derrick, was throwing a big back to school party the next night, and that everyone expected them to be there. Chad was excited about the party, because he hadn't seen any of his school friends in a week. The next night when Chad and Katherine arrived at the party, it was just like it had always been, everyone went crazy and started giving him high fives, and asking him about basketball, and then something happened that never happened before, someone offered Chad a beer, and he said no thanks. Derrick came over and asked Chad what was up. He had never seen Chad turn down a beer before. He thought maybe Chad had to get up early, or had to leave the party early. There had to be a good reason. Chad would not just not drink. Chad then told Derrick all the things that he told Katherine the day before. Derrick didn't believe it, but said if that was what Chad wanted to do, then best of luck, but he was going to get wasted enough for the both of them. At first, Chad was having a good time, catching up with his buddies, and listening to stories, but then as he looked around, and saw all of his friends in a drunken stupor, he became sad. Chad never saw it from that point of view before, he was usually the biggest fish in the pond, but now he just thought it was stupid, and wanted to leave. He told Derrick thanks for inviting him and Katherine to the party, but that they would now be leaving. Katherine was at a loss too. She thought maybe he had to be home because of his father, but when he told her he just didn't want to be around all the drinking, and other stuff that was going on, she got mad. Katherine didn't know why he had to ruin her good time, just because he found religion. She told him to take her back, and said she would find a ride home with one of her girlfriends. That really hurt Chad's feelings, but he did as she asked, and told her to please be careful, and not ride home with anyone who was drunk. She promised, and then he drove home alone. That was the first time that Chad and Katherine ever went somewhere together but left separately. He was proud of himself though, because he passed another test of his faith. The first test was when he was alone with Katherine at the house the day before, and now he had turned down alcohol. Chad had never turned down either one before. Chad thanked God for giving him the strength to do the right things. He then asked for further strength, because he knew now, that he had a hard road ahead of him, and couldn't do it alone.

The next day Katherine called to let him know that she made it home safely, and that she was sorry for how she acted. She just didn't want to leave early, because it was the last weekend before school started. Chad told her he understood, and that he was not mad at her, and that he would talk to her later that night.

Chad had been home two days, and still hadn't even seen his parents. His dad had been out of town on business, and his mother was never home when he was, because of her job. Finally they were both home, so he asked them if he could talk to them. They too, like Katherine, thought maybe he had come to a decision on college, but he let them know that was not it, but something much more important. That led his father to say, "Nothing is more important than school, and you better not have gotten that girlfriend of yours pregnant." Chad assured him that was not the case, and that he just wanted to let them know that he got saved while he was at church camp. His father was less than thrilled, and acted as if Chad wasted his precious time he could have spent watching the baseball game on television. His mother just said, that's nice dear, and went back to looking at papers she brought home from work. Chad thought everyone was going to be excited or at least happy for him, but it seemed that nobody cared. Now reality was starting to hit Chad in the face. Outside of the people at camp, and the people at Jordan's church, where he was now going to attend, not a single person cared about his feelings. If he announced he was going to play for the state college, everyone would throw him a party, but since he only got saved, it's just a nice thing. He was discouraged, but he was not about to give up without a fight. He was going to show everyone that there was something to it, and he didn't care if it took him the rest of his life to do so.

Chapter III
Back To School

    Today was the first day of school, and Chad was looking forward to it. He was a Senior now, and he knew that this would be a year of many great things for him personally. He would be choosing a college to play basketball for, he was exactly 300 points away from breaking the state record for all time points scored in a career, and he even had a great chance of being ranked number one nationally for all basketball prospects. Chad also wanted to do something that his school hadn't been able to achieve in 17 years, and that was winning the state championship. He came within a few games of doing that last year, but his team was eliminated in the Semi State on a last second shot. Chad worked hard all summer on his game, and now he was ready to hit the shot to win it for his school.

    Chad left his house early that day so that he could talk with his coach before school. When he got there, Coach Bush gave him his usual stack of letters from schools trying to persuade him to come to their school. Chad had not narrowed his list down to 5, or even 10, but he knew he wasn't going anywhere where his friends and family couldn't come watch him play. He also knew it was time to make a list of schools, and start taking visits to those schools to see which he felt was the best fit for him. Chad knew he needed to find a coach he liked, and could respect. Chad also wanted to go somewhere that would give him a chance of winning a national championship. More important than anything else, the school needed to offer him an opportunity to excel academically. He knew if for some reason he didn't make it to the pros, he would need a good education to fall back on. Chad told

Coach Bush that he would have a list of 5 schools by the end of the week, and that he would like for him to turn that list in to the media for him. Coach Bush gladly agreed, and told Chad if he needed any help, he could call or visit him whenever he wanted. Chad thanked him, and headed to his first class for the day.

The first day of school was usually one filled with more socializing than actual learning. Everyone wanted to catch up with their friends, and share what all they did over the summer. Chad thought this would be a great time to share with his buddies what had happened to him at church camp, and invite them to come to church with him. He quickly was reminded of how it was when Jordan use to invite him. People were saying "Thanks, but no thanks." The funny thing was that they seemed to use the same excuses he used, "I'm busy that night" or when he asked if they could come Sunday morning, if not through the week, they said they didn't get to sleep in on any other day, so they wanted to catch up on their sleep. Chad thought to himself that it was only the first day, so maybe by the end of the week, someone would go with him. He knew it wasn't going to be easy, but he also knew that it was important to keep trying.

When he got home from school that day, he told his father that he was ready to make a list of five schools and that he would like his input on things. Chad would never have asked his father to help him before, but he knew he needed to work on their relationship, so he made the first move. After about an hour of going over the schools he liked, and weighing the pros and cons of each one, he successfully narrowed his list to five. Then he began making phone calls to those schools, and to all the other schools that had showed so much interest in him to let them know that he was no longer considering them for his services, but he wanted to thank them for their interest. The main school that Chad was interested in was the state school that was just a short drive from home. The school had already won several National Championships over the years, and looked to be in good shape to do it again. The team was loaded with several All Americans, and had already signed two more from Chad's class. They told Chad that they had one more scholarship left, and that they would hold it for him if he would give them a verbal commitment. Chad grew up a fan of the team, but he thought he owed it to himself, and to the other schools to see what they had to offer him by way of basketball and academics. One big problem with the other schools he had before even visiting them was that not one of them was located in Indiana. Two schools were located in North Carolina, one in Kentucky, and the other was in Texas. Chad always said he was going to stay close to home, but the schools were all amazing academically and contenders every year for the National Title. Chad wasn't sure what to do. His dad wanted him to choose the state school for the obvious reasons of being a fan, and the proximity to home, but Chad knew this decision was the second biggest one of his life thus far, and wanted to make sure when he gave his commitment, that he was 100% positive it was the best fit for him. He was glad that tomorrow was Wednesday, and that he could sit and talk with his new pastor about it.

The next day at school everyone already knew from Katherine that Chad had made his list, and who the schools were, so everyone who liked one school better than the other made sure they let him know where they thought he should go, even the faculty. Chad was polite, and thanked them for their input, but he was very weary of it all. The sooner he could get it over with, the better. That night after church, Chad went to his pastors' home and told him all of his feelings, and asked him for his advice. His pastor told him that he would assist him if he could, but that the decision should be made after praying about it, and talking it over with his parents. He assured Chad that God would show him which one was the right one after he took his visits. He then prayed with Chad, and promised that he would continue to pray for him until he made the choice. Chad felt much better about everything after that, and when he got home he phoned all the coaches involved and set up his visits.

Chad knew his final high school basketball season was just around the corner, and he needed to get all of this behind him so he could focus. It was September now, and he had until November to take the visits, give his verbal, work on all of the goals he set for the team, and himself. It was going to be an extremely busy, yet fun couple of months.

Chapter IV
The Visits

Chad and his father decided that they would first visit the two North Carolina schools. The schools were less than fifty miles apart, and they could visit them both in one weekend. Chad had always been aware of the two schools, and respected them as institutions of learning, and fantastic basketball programs. They were both rich in basketball tradition, and only recruited the best of the best. When they started recruiting Chad, it was the confirmation that he had been waiting for his whole life that he truly was among the elite in high school basketball. He and his father would be leaving for North Carolina following his final class on Thursday, so that he could spend three days looking around, and trying to get a feel if either of the schools felt right for him. He never thought he would go that far from home, but he decided if he felt led by the Lord to go to either school, he would do so. One major obstacle would be Katherine. She wouldn't be able to attend either of the schools in North Carolina because they were both very expensive, and since she would be an out of state student, it would cost even more for her, so he knew that if he chose one of them, it would put a tremendous strain on their relationship, if not destroy it completely. He decided not to worry about it, and just leave it up to God, because He alone is in control.

By the time Thursday came around, Chad was about to burst. He couldn't wait to get out of school and start his visits. Immediately after class let out, his father was picking him up, and then they were off to the airport. The day went by so slow that he felt like he was in prison serving a life term, but then it happened, the final bell rang, and he was off.

Chad had never flown before, because he had always been afraid to, but now that he knew he was going to Heaven if his plane should happen to crash, he wasn't scared at all. Also he knew he had to fly because it would take too long to drive North Carolina, which would also cut into his time on campus. When the plane took off, Chad said a little prayer to himself and tried to relax. Then he found out something he would never have believed until it happened, he actually liked flying! He got to sit by the window, which was amazing to him how small everything looked, and how beautiful it was to see from above the clouds. The plane was also playing a movie that he wanted to see, so that made it even better.

When they arrived in North Carolina, the coach from the first school was there to meet him. Coach Kennedy was believed by everyone in basketball circles to be the best coach in college basketball. He ran a clean program, and graduated players. As far as Chad knew, the only thing bad about the coach or his school was that it was a long way from home. Coach Kennedy took them personally to their hotel, and told them to get some rest because it would be a busy day for them tomorrow.

The next morning they got up, had breakfast, and were taken to meet the coach on campus. The first thing they did when they arrived was to visit the arena where the team practiced, and played games. It was a small arena, but that was the beauty of it. Every team that came to play there hated it, because the fans were right on top of the court, and they were always getting all over the players from the opposing team. Chad then met some of the players on the team. All the guys were very friendly, and treated Chad like he was already on the team. After looking around and shooting a few baskets, the guys all took Chad to a local restaurant. Chad was amazed that the people there knew who he was. He even signed a few autographs. He was use to doing that in Indiana, but he never dreamed that people in North Carolina would know about him. He was thoroughly enjoying his first visit, but he knew he had four others to take before making that final choice. When he and his father got back to the hotel that night, he was exhausted, it had been a long day, and he had to get some rest for tomorrow's visit.

The next day Chad and his father rented a car, and drove to the other N.C. school. Not to be outdone, Coach Wallace had a lot of things going for him at his school. They had a new state of the art arena and a separate facility for practices. The school had won their share of championships, even though he himself had just won one, but that one, was just two years ago. The campus was beautiful, and the players there were all unbelievably talented. No other program had turned out more professionals than this school. The school also had a good history of graduating players. Usually the only players who didn't graduate, were the ones who left school early to play professionally, and many of them eventually came back to get their degree later. Chad and his father were having a great time, and when it came time for them to go back to Indiana, they talked about the two visits. Chad asked his dad if he would be very upset if when it came time to pick a school, if he chose one of the N.C. schools. To his surprise, he said no, but he wouldn't be caught dead wearing any of their shirts around town, because all the fans of the home school would shoot him. They both laughed, and watched the movie. When they arrived back home, his mother and Katherine were there waiting for them. Chad was glad that Katherine was there, he wanted to talk to her about the trip. He decided not to say too much though, because he didn't want her to worry about him being so far away, and he still had three more visits to take. For all he knew, he might like one of the remaining schools better.

Chad planned on taking the visit to the school in Kentucky the following weekend. He didn't have to fly or miss any classes. He could just wait for school to get out and then drive down there. The week passed by swiftly, and it was now time to leave for Kentucky. Chad didn't take his father this time. Instead, he went with his friend Derrick.

Derrick had always been a big fan of the team in Kentucky, so Chad thought it would be a nice gesture if he invited him along. Derrick accepted gladly, and the two of them left following their final classes. When Chad and Derrick arrived at the university, it was much different from the visit to the other schools. This time the coach came with all the players, the cheerleaders and even the pep band. Coach Sanders was trying to pull out every trick he knew to land Chad, because his team was only one special player away from being a contender for the championship. The first stop was once again the arena where the team played. The coach showed Chad the banners from their previous victories, and told him that with his help, there could be a few more hanging up there.

Then the coach took the boys out to a local favorite restaurant of the players and the kids on campus. At the end of the night, the coach told the two boys that they could stay with some players on the team instead of staying at a hotel. Chad and Derrick accepted, and followed the players back to their apartment.

When they got there, the guys had a huge party waiting on them. Derrick was pumped, he couldn't believe he was going to be partying with college basketball players, but Chad was extremely uncomfortable. There was a lot of drinking, and not only that, but the guys from the team had arranged for some of the cheerleaders to come too. The girls were all beautiful, and they were not exactly moral.

They were there to try and show Chad a good time, and convince him that he should come to their school. Chad tried to tell them he had a girlfriend that he loved, but they assured him that they wouldn't tell, nor was she there, so it would be okay. Derrick didn't help the situation either, he had already downed a few beers, and he told Chad he wouldn't tell Katherine anything. Derrick then told Chad that he would have to be a fool to turn down girls that hot. Chad was tempted, but he refused their advances. He told the girls that he had a girlfriend that he loved, and that he was a Christian, and being a Christian he didn't believe in having sex with anyone that was not his wife. One of the girls told Chad that she was a Christian too, but she didn't see anything wrong with drinking, or having sex, and that he should just have a good time. Chad was furious! How could this girl claim to be a Christian, and still do everything that the world did? He knew it wasn't his place to judge her, but it made him angry and at the same time very sad. Chad told the guys thanks for having him over, but he would feel more comfortable at a hotel. Derrick wanted to stay, but he knew that he was only able to be there because of Chad, so he left with him.

The next day the boys got up early and left for home. Derrick was sulking all the way back. He didn't know why Chad had to ruin everything because of his religious beliefs. He didn't have to leave. He could have hung out with everyone. Chad apologized, and told Derrick that he had to leave because it was a temptation, and he didn't want to be in that kind of environment. Derrick didn't care, he was mad because he was trying to hook up with one of the girls there, and he didn't get to because of Chad. When the boys got home, Derrick didn't say thank you or anything at all. He just got in his car and left. Chad thought he was doing his friend a favor by taking him along on a recruiting visit, but all he got for his effort was grief. Chad thought to himself that he wouldn't ask any friends to go from now on, just his dad.

The next trip was planned for the school in Texas the following weekend, but something on the news changed all of that. The coach from the university he was going to visit announced that he was retiring after the season. Chad was only considering that college because of the coach, now he knew he didn't want to go there. Chad called the coach that night, and let him know that he would not be making the trip, but thanked him for recruiting him.

Now Chad was just down to one final school to visit, and it was the school everyone wanted him to attend, the school from Indiana. After getting off of the phone with the coach from Texas, he phoned the coach appointed for his last scheduled visit. Chad informed him that he was not going to be taking the Texas visit, and wanted to know if he could move the visit to his school, up a week. The coach was more than happy to entertain him a week earlier, and told him not only could he come a week earlier, but he was welcome to come every day if he liked. Coach Samuel was a very congenial guy. Everyone in the media, and coaching ranks liked, and respected him immensely. Chad was looking forward to the final visit and getting it all behind him.

All week at school everyone told Chad how great it would be if he chose the home school and how much fun it would be to be able to watch him play in person, and not have to watch him on television only. There was a lot of pressure being put on him from all sides.

When the weekend came, Chad and his father drove the short trip to the university and met with the coach. It was different from the other trips, because Coach Samuel wasn't trying to sell Chad on the school. Instead, he sat and talked with them and told Chad how he envisioned him fitting in his system, and that he thought he could help him reach his full potential as a person and a player. Coach Samuel was also a Christian, and he had very strict rules and guidelines that the players had to follow. He made sure they went to class, that they were in their dorm by eleven every night, and that they were respectable members of the community. Coach Samuel wasn't flashy, he was just genuine, and both Chad and his father liked that very much. Chad was ready to commit right then, but knew he needed to go home and talk it over with his pastor and pray about it first.

When Chad got home, he phoned his pastor, and then went to see him. He told his pastor that he thought he was ready to make his decision, and wanted to know if he would pray with him first. After praying, Chad knew in his heart that the best fit for him in every way was the home school. It had a coach who was a Christian, it was close to home, and being close to home, it would allow him to still attend his own church. It was perfect. Not only was it good because of it's location, but it was a program that had won five championships in the past, and with the team they had now, plus the addition of Chad the next year, they would have a great chance to win another one.

Unlike so many of the top players, Chad didn't hold a big flashy press conference with media, and television reporters, he just simply called the coaches he didn't choose, thanked them, and informed them that he would not be coming to their school. Then Chad called Coach Samuel, and informed him that he would be signing a National Letter of Intent with him during the early signing period. Chad was very excited about getting his choice behind him. He could now start focusing on getting ready for the season and accomplishing his goals.

Chapter V
Tragedy

One of the first people Chad wanted to tell about his decision was his friend Jordan. Jordan was not only one of his best friends, but he was also a life long fan of the team Chad gave his verbal commitment to. When Chad called Jordan and told him the news, he told Chad that he better not be joking, and if he wasn't, that he better introduce him to all the guys on the team, and Coach Samuel. Chad laughed, and promised he would, and that he would also give him the best tickets he could get his hands on when his team gets into the NCAA Tournament. Jordan was elated. He told Chad that he was coming home for Thanksgiving, and that he wanted to hang out the whole break with him. Chad said he would have to spend some time with his family and Katherine, but he would definitely spend as much time with him as possible.

Chad was happy that he was going to be able to see his friend again. Jordan had been gone for a few months now, and hadn't been able to come home because he was attending a school on the other side of the country. Jordan was really the only Christian friend Chad had. There were a lot of people his age at his new church, but the ones he knew there, didn't try to live a Christian life. They wore Christian shirts, necklaces with a cross on it, and told everyone that they were Christians, but they were promiscuous, got drunk every weekend, and the only time they attended church was on Sunday morning, because they were too busy doing everything else on Sunday night, and Wednesday night. Jesus was great and all, but he was never the first priority, or even second. Chad knew Jordan was different, because he was around Jordan before he was saved, and Jordan had never been anything other than a witness, and an example of how a Christian should act. He never once drank alcohol, did drugs, or even curse. Also, Jordan was not ashamed of the fact that he was a virgin. He even let everyone know that he planned on staying that way until he was married. Chad use to make fun of him for being a virgin, now he admired him for it. After talking a while, Chad asked Jordan if he could pick him up from the airport when he came home. Jordan said that would be great and that it would give them a chance to catch up on the drive home.

Chad was really looking forward to it. Since Thanksgiving was coming up, the school week ended on Wednesday. That meant that Chad could pick up Jordan, and the two of them could go to church together that night when they got home. It had been storming the whole day, and Chad was worried about Jordan arriving safely, but thankfully the flight made it in without any trouble. Jordan was the first one to come out of the tunnel. Chad asked Jordan if he was scared at all flying home in the storm. Jordan said he was nervous at first, but then he put his head down, closed his eyes and prayed, and then he was better after that. Chad let him know he had prayed for him too. Jordan thanked him and the two started on their way to the car.

As they got to the car, the rain started coming down even harder than before. Chad didn't like driving in traffic as it was, and now it was made even worse by the fact that his vision was impaired by all the rain. He asked Jordan if he thought they should pull over and wait it out, or just continue towards home. Jordan said he wanted to go on, because he hadn't been able to attend his own church for such a long time, and if they waited it out, who knew how long it might last. Chad agreed, so the two boys continued on their way.

They were just a few miles from home when a car from the

other lane lost control, slid across to their side, and hit them head on. Chad was wearing his seatbelt, but Jordan was not. Chad was knocked unconscious and seriously injured. Jordan was thrown from the car and killed instantly. When Chad awoke, he was in the hospital. The first thing he wanted to know was if Jordan was okay. His father had to tell him the horrible news. Jordan didn't make it. Chad didn't believe him. Jordan couldn't be dead, he just couldn't be! He couldn't believe that God would let Jordan die. God knew how much Chad depended on Jordan for advice and friendship, He couldn't take him away! There was more bad news. The injuries that Chad sustained in the wreck were going to cost him his chance to play for the first few weeks of the basketball season. Now, not only had he lost his closest friend, but it looked like he wouldn't be able to achieve his goals to be the all-time leading scorer in state history, be named Mr. Basketball for his state, or National Player of the year.

Chad didn't understand why all of this had to happen. He thought he was living the life that God wanted him to live. He was going to church, he was witnessing to people and he was doing everything he knew to do. Chad didn't understand, but when he was alone that night, he prayed and told God that although he didn't understand why things were going wrong, that he trusted Him, and wanted whatever the Lord had planned for his life to come to pass. He also told God that he was thankful for the time he did have with Jordan on Earth, and that he knew Jordan was in a better place now. After Chad prayed, he felt at peace, and had a good nights rest.

The next day was Thanksgiving and Katherine came to visit him in the hospital. Katherine was initially there to be supportive and cheer him up, but when Chad started telling her how thankful he was to be alive, and how good God is to him in all things, Katherine became very angry. She asked Chad how he could lay there in a hospital bed, when he should be home with his family and friends celebrating the holiday, having lost his best friend in the same accident that put him in the hospital, and then tell her how good God is. Katherine said that if this is what God does for you, then she didn't want any part of God or being a Christian. Chad was extremely hurt by her statement, and told her that maybe they should take some time apart for a while. Katherine told him she could make it even easier, and said she was done trying at all. She wasn't happy, and hadn't been happy since he came back from camp. She gave him his class ring, and left his room. Chad knew that it was for the best. Katherine had been the love of his life before he met Christ, and when Jesus took her place, she never accepted it. She wanted the old Chad, the one who was the life of the party, drank alcohol, and didn't have rules about having sex before marriage. Chad had always believed that he would eventually get through to Katherine, and that the two could share the life that God intended for couples, but now it appeared that dream was over too. Chad knew that if God wanted him to be with Katherine, that they would work it out, and that she would come to Christ just as he did, but if it wasn't meant for them to be together, then God had another girl for him, and he would find her when the time was right.

That night Chad just strengthened himself by reading his Bible, and praying. He wasn't going to give up on his goals, even if he did have a major setback. He believed God had a purpose for everything that happened in his life, and that he would somehow use this tragedy for Gods' glory in some way or another.

The next few days at the hospital, Chad shared his faith with all the doctors, nurses, and fellow patients he came in contact with. He never complained about the bad break he got, about the food, or the tests he had to take. Chad was quickly becoming the favorite patient of the whole staff. Nurses brought him treats regularly, and made sure he was comfortable and happy at all times. Doctors would come in and swap jokes with him, and tell him how much they enjoyed watching him play basketball. Chad had only been in the hospital a week when the doctor informed him that he was healing much faster than anticipated, and that he would be able to go home and be released to play basketball immediately. The doctor credited the speedy recovery to the fact that Chad was young, and a superb athletic specimen, but Chad gave all the credit to God. He believed he was healed, and that God was once again proving to him that if he would just trust Him that everything would work out for the best. Chad could hardly wait to get back to school, and in the gym. He had only missed a few practices, and would be able to join the team in time to play their first game. All of his hopes and dreams were back in place. Chad decided that he would dedicate the season to the memory of his friend Jordan, and even changed his number to the one Jordan wore. He was determined more than ever to achieve every last goal he had before the wreck and do it all to the glory of God.

Chapter VI
The Season Begins

The first day back to school for Chad was a hectic one. Every student he passed in the hall, or had a class with, asked him if he was going to be able to play basketball in time for the first game. The ones who didn't ask him about that, asked him about his breakup with Katherine. Chad also had a weeks worth of homework to take home after basketball practice. It was not a good day by any means, not only was he extremely behind in his school work, but now he didn't have Katherine to talk to, or help him get caught up. She had always been there before no matter what the crisis, now she wouldn't talk, or even look at him. Chad knew he couldn't dwell on the negative and that he had to get ready for basketball. The first game was a few days away, and he wasn't feeling mentally, or physically ready to play. He knew it didn't matter how he felt, because when the game arrived he had to go out there, and perform like his old self. His team depended on him.

Chad went to practice the day before the game and worked on sharpening his skills and conditioning. He shot five hundred extra shots, and ran wind sprints for an hour after everyone else went home. The next day was the first big test to see what kind of progress he had made in his short time back.

For the opening game of the year, Chad and his team were set to play a team from Bloomington, who was ranked in the top ten in the state. The team featured Greg Gordon, who was also considered to be a top prospect nationally, and was the main competition for Chad in the states' coveted Mr. Basketball award. Chad had always hated Greg before, and the two almost got into a fight last year, but now Chad knew he couldn't act that way any longer because he is a Christian.

Before the game, Chad went up to Greg, and wished him good luck, and offered to shake his hand, but Greg refused it, and told Chad he wasn't fooling him, and accused him of just trying to win votes. Chad then resorted to his old self, and told Greg that he didn't need to politic to get votes, and that his game was all he needed to beat a no talent loser like him! As the game got under way, Chad was unstoppable. He scored his teams' first ten points. By halftime, Chad had twenty points, and his team led by ten points. Greg had only managed to score six points, and Chad had been talking trash to him about it the whole game. Chad told him that he wasn't even good enough to be on the same floor with him, and that maybe he should just quit playing all together.

During halftime, Derrick leaned over to Chad and told him how great it was that he wasn't different when it came to basketball. Chad asked him what he meant. Derrick said he just meant that when he became a Christian he had quit doing all the stuff he use to do, but at least when it came to basketball, he was still cocky and talked trash to that jerk on the other team. That was when Chad realized he messed up. Immediately he told God he was sorry, and that he would try not to do it ever again. Chad knew he was not being a good witness to Derrick, nor to the guy he was playing against. The rest of the game Chad just played and didn't talk at all. His team won, and Chad scored thirty points but he wasn't happy.

After the game, Chad waited on Greg to come out of the locker room. When Chad finally saw Greg, he went up to him and apologized for being a jerk, and wished him a great season. Greg could tell he was sincere, and graciously accepted his apology, and offered one of his own to Chad. Chad then went to Derrick, and told him he was sorry that he lost his cool, and that he was glad that Derrick had pointed out his mistake to him. Derrick couldn't believe what he was hearing. He thought it was great to have some part of the old Chad still around and now that too was going to be gone. He told Chad that he was a fanatic, and that he needed to chill with all the Jesus stuff. Chad knew he was doing the right thing though, and if he had to lose every friend he had before he got saved, in order to be a good Christian, he would do it without any regrets.

The next night, Chad had another game. The game was a road game, and Chad was a little anxious about what some fans might say to him. He had been the target of opposing teams' student cheering sections many times in previous years, and he knew how ruthless they could be with what they would shout at him. Before the game, Chad said a prayer that the Lord would give him grace to ignore the ravings of some fan who is trying to get in his head, and that he would protect Chad, and all the participants on both teams. After his prayer, Chad and his team ran out of the locker room into a very hostile and frenzied crowd. Immediately the crowd started heckling Chad. Most of the shouts were "You Suck!", or "Over-Rated", but that wasn't too bad, Chad was use to hearing those over the years, but then he heard one that infuriated and hurt him almost to the point of tears. One of the kids in the student section yelled at him about his wreck and about Jordan.

When Chad heard that, he wanted to go after the guy, but instead, he went to his coach and informed him what was said. Coach Bush was enraged. He went to the coach on the other team and told him to get the Athletic Director and that either they throw the kid out who made the remark, or they would not be playing tonight. The opposing teams' coach and the A.D. agreed that it was the right decision, and escorted the young man out of the gym. This move really got the student section in an uproar. They were on Chad all game, calling him a cry baby, along with all the other things that were already being shouted. Chad struggled at first, and was even concerned about his safety, but then he remembered that he wasn't out there alone, and that God would protect him. After that, Chad started playing like his old self. He even started playing with the crowd. Chad scored thirty-five points, and led his team to a victory once again.

After the game Chad went to the Athletic Director and asked him to deliver a message for him. The Athletic Director said he would, and asked who the message was for, and what the message was. Chad asked him to tell the kid who was ejected from the game that he was sorry that he had him thrown out, and that he forgave him for saying what he said. The Athletic Director couldn't understand why Chad would do that, but said he would relay the message. Chad knew that sometimes people yell things at games, that they wouldn't normally say. It wasn't acceptable, but it definitely was something he could, and would forgive. Chad was just happy that he was able to overcome the initial feeling of anger and do the right thing. He was also happy that his team won, and he nearly scored forty points. The next day was Sunday, and usually after back to back games on the weekend, Chad enjoyed sleeping in on Sunday, but now he looked forward to getting up, and going to church. Chad just wished that the kids at church would be like the kids at camp, and be serious about God. Even though he knew the Lord was with him, he still longed for friends his age that he could talk to and share with.

Chapter VII

New People At Church

On Sunday morning when Chad walked into his Sunday School class, he noticed that there were two new people, a brother and sister. Chad walked over to them, introduced himself, and asked them their names, ages, and where they were from. The boy spoke up first. He said his name was Reece Fleetwood, he was 18, and his sisters' name was Rachel, and she was 16. Their fathers' job was transferred from Tennessee to Indiana, and they would be starting at Chad's school on Monday. Chad told Reece that if he could help him, or his sister in any way, to let him know. He would love to show them around school, or the town, if they wished. Reece thanked him, and said he would most definitely take him up on that offer tomorrow at school. Chad wasn't sure yet, but he was hoping that this new family was the answer to his prayers. He wouldn't know for sure though, until he could see how they acted outside of church, and around other kids.

    The next morning, Chad waited for Reece and Rachel to arrive at school. He got permission from the principal to be their personal guide for the first few days, until they knew their way around. Reece and Rachel were relieved to see Chad was sincere about helping them, and not just saying it to sound nice. As he was showing them around the school, Reece noticed that everyone they passed in the hallway almost broke their neck to say hi to them. He asked Chad if everyone was always so friendly. Chad said no, and explained that most of the kids were friendly to him because he plays basketball, but he didn't tell him that he was considered by most analysts to be the number one basketball recruit in the country. He didn't want Reece, or Rachel to know about that if he could keep it from them. He wanted them to either like, or dislike him because of who he was, not how good he was at putting a leather ball through an iron hoop. This was the first time someone in his town didn't know who he was since he was 13, and he liked the idea of not wondering if they liked him, or if they just wanted to go along for the ride.

As the day went by and Chad continued to show the two around, he kept finding himself flirting with Rachel. She was an absolutely beautiful girl and she had the cutest accent he had ever heard. He wanted to ask her out, but he knew it was too soon. He needed to know more about her. Was she a strong Christian or was she just another poser? He intended to find out. As the week went by, and Chad got to know Reece and Rachel better, he liked them more and more. On Wednesday, he asked them if their family would be at church, and they said they never missed church unless they were sick, or they were out of town. Chad was glad to hear that and told them he would see them there. That night after church, Chad asked Reece if he could call Rachel sometime, or would it upset him. Reece laughed and told Chad he wished that he would call Rachel, because all she ever talked about was how cute Chad was. Chad was relieved that Reece wouldn't care, and was excited that Rachel also found him attractive. Then Chad asked Reece if he and Rachel would be at the game Friday. Reece said they were coming for sure. As soon as he finished talking to Reece, he went up to Rachel and asked her if she would like to go eat with him after the game Friday, and go on a date Saturday. Rachel turned red, and said she would love to do both.

The next day at school Chad walked Rachel to every class. He marveled at how a girl as beautiful as Rachel could be so sweet and humble at the same time. Every time he told her how pretty she was, she just turned red, and said thank you in that cute little accent of hers. That night Chad talked to Rachel on the phone for hours. He found himself quickly forgetting all about Katherine, and started to fall hard for Rachel. She was everything he thought a girl should be, and couldn't wait until Friday and Saturday night.

Before the game Friday, Chad found a note on his car from Rachel. The note wished him luck, and said she didn't care if he won or lost, but she was praying that he and the other boys would be safe. It also said she was looking forward to seeing him after the game. Chad told himself that at the game tonight, he was going to put on a show. Reece and Rachel had never experienced what basketball was like in Indiana, and for their first game he was going to explode.

That night, as soon as the game got under way, Chad took the opening tip down the floor, and threw it home with a thunderous dunk! The crowd erupted with a cheer, but Chad was just getting started. Chad did something that night that he had never done before, he scored 57 points. The most he had ever scored before was 44, which is still unthinkable by most, but this night was special. Chad's team won again, keeping his team undefeated, and his 57 points moved him to third on the list for career points scored. He was only 50 points away from second, and 179 points away from owning it.

After the game Reece and Rachel told Chad that he was awesome, and that he should play in college. It was then that Chad let them in on the secret everyone else already knew, he was going to play in college. Chad explained that he didn't tell them before because he didn't want to brag, and he wanted to see how they would treat him as just a regular person and not a superstar. Reece and Rachel said they understood. They were happy and excited that he would be able to continue playing basketball after high school. Chad then told Rachel that he would take a quick shower so they could go get something to eat. Rachel said she was more than happy to wait, because he needed a shower, and laughed.

    That night, as Chad and Rachel spent time together, Chad experienced what it was that he had been looking for since he gave his life to Christ. He was spending time with a girl, having good, clean fun, and never once had a thought about sex. When he took Rachel home, Chad didn't even kiss her goodnight, but did give her a hug bye. As he was driving home, Chad got a text on his cell phone, it was from Rachel, it said that she just wanted to thank him for showing her a great time, and that she was really excited about tomorrows' date. Chad was looking forward to it too, and was grateful that the Lord had brought the Fleetwood family to his town and church.

    The next morning, Chad called Rachel and asked if she could be ready around noon, because he wanted to spend the whole day with her. Rachel said she could be, and liked the idea of spending the day with him too. On the way to Rachel's house, Chad first stopped at the florists and bought three roses, one red, one white, and one pink, he then went to pick up Rachel. When Chad arrived, and gave the roses to Rachel, she said they were beautiful, and that it was very sweet of him to buy her roses, but why the three different colors. Chad explained that each one had a meaning, and then he told her the meaning of each. The white rose was for purity, and he wanted her to know that his intentions were pure. The pink rose was for friendship, and that no matter what happened, he hoped they would always remain friends. Then he told her that the red rose was for love, and that he hoped that their relationship would eventually blossom into love. Rachel told Chad that she thought what he said was beautiful and poetic. Then she gave him a big hug and a kiss on the cheek. Chad was happy that she was pleased, and asked her if she was ready to go. Rachel said she wanted to put her beautiful roses in a vase and water first, and then she would be.

The whole date, Chad kept thinking how great it was to be with a girl like Rachel. She loved God, she was drop-dead gorgeous, and she was fun to be with. He knew that he was ready to ask her if she would be his and his alone. When it came time to take Rachel home, Chad walked her to the door and asked her if she would just date him, and nobody else. Rachel said if he wouldn't have asked her, she was going to ask him that same question, and they both laughed. Chad said he wished he would have waited on her now, but he was glad they were feeling the same way. Then he kissed her gently on the lips, and gave her a hug good-bye.

All the way home, Chad kept telling God how grateful and thankful he was that he put Rachel in his life and that he wanted to put their relationship in his hands.

Chapter VIII
Katherine

    Everything was starting to fall into place for Chad. He felt that he was in Gods' will, his basketball game had never been better, and he now had a girlfriend who felt the same way he did about God, and the manner in which you are to behave when you are dating. Unfortunately, not everyone saw things the way Chad did, and it appeared that they were going to do everything they could to ruin his new found happiness.

    One day, as Chad was waiting for Rachel at her locker, he saw Rachel coming down the hall crying. Immediately Chad ran up to Rachel, and asked her about what was upsetting her to the point of tears. At first Rachel said she didn't want to talk about it, and that she would be fine, but Chad persisted. After a few minutes, Rachel finally gave in and explained that Katherine had been making fun of her for how she talked, how she dressed, and telling her that she would never be good enough for Chad, or know how to please him the way that she did. After Chad heard this, he told Rachel that he was going to set Katherine straight and that he wouldn't let Katherine treat her that way. Rachel told Chad that she would prefer if he wouldn't say anything to her at all, because it would only cause more trouble and that she would be okay. Chad reluctantly agreed, but said if he heard about any further instances, he was going to have a talk with Katherine. Rachel said she was embarrassed about crying and that she didn't want to cause any trouble, but Katherine was just so mean and it really hurt her feelings. She didn't understand why Katherine was acting this way, because Katherine had broke it off with Chad, and all of that was before Rachel had even moved to town. Chad said Katherine was acting that way to get attention, and that she felt threatened by Rachel because everyone thought she was so nice and pretty. Rachel still didn't understand. She didn't have any bad feelings towards Katherine; she would even like to be her friend. Chad told her that the odds of that happening were slim to none, but just her saying that was further proof of how Rachel was heads and shoulders above every other girl. Rachel blushed, and told him they had better get to class before the bell, but talking to him made her feel better. She then made Chad promise one more time that he wouldn't say anything to Katherine about any of what she told him. Chad promised, but made sure Rachel knew that if Katherine did, or said anything else, he was not going to keep silent. With that said, the two left for class.

Chad couldn't concentrate the rest of the day. He wanted to tell Katherine off, but he knew a promise was a promise, and he also knew that telling her off wouldn't accomplish anything except adding fuel to the fire. Katherine didn't need anyone to add fuel to her fire, she had already decided that she was either going to break Chad and Rachel up, or make their lives miserable. For the rest of the week she tormented Rachel, calling her names, and threatening her with acts of violence. Rachel didn't tell Chad though, because she didn't want Chad to say anything, so she just took the abuse, and battled through it.

As the weekend arrived Chad was a little bummed. He had two basketball games, but neither game was at his school. Chad didn't even want to see Katherine, and now he was going to be stuck riding a school bus with her two nights in a row. Also, neither game was close to home, so that meant he would be getting home late and therefore no date with Rachel either night. At least Rachel's parents agreed to let her and Reece ride to the games with Chad's parents. All the way to the game Katherine kept trying to sit by Chad and talk to him. Chad asked her why she was all of a sudden interested in him again. She was the one who broke it off with him and she knew it wouldn't work now that he was a Christian. Katherine told Chad that she knew that she made a mistake that day and that she would be willing to work things out with him if he would give her another chance. She would even come to church with him. Chad told Katherine that she was welcome to come to church with him anytime, but he was very happy with Rachel and that he didn't see himself ever dating her again. Katherine stormed away and sat with the cheerleaders.

That night at the game Chad went up against a coach who was determined to shut him down. They played junk defenses on him, and on offense they stalled. Chad only scored 19 points that night, but his team won. That was the most important thing.

On the way home Chad tried to sleep, but he was awakened by feeling a kiss on his lips. It was Katherine. Chad asked her what she thought she was doing. Katherine said she just wanted to remind him of what he was missing and that she knew that the "Virgin Queen" probably didn't even know how to kiss. Chad told Katherine once again that it wasn't about physical stuff with him anymore, and that Rachel was better than Katherine in every aspect of being a girlfriend, and that she needed to get it through her head that it is over for good. Katherine then cussed him out and told him he could keep his little prude girlfriend.

The next day Chad told Rachel what happened and assured her that she was the one he wanted, and not Katherine. Rachel didn't doubt him, but she did doubt that Katherine would finally leave them alone. The next morning when Rachel and her family went outside, there was trash all over their lawn, eggs smashed all over their house and cars, and toilet paper in their trees. It was obvious who did it, but there was no way to prove it. When Chad found out, he went to

Rachel's house to help clean up, and apologize to her parents that his ex-girlfriend was psychotic. Rachel's parents were extremely angry, and wanted to call the police, but they knew they didn't have any proof as to who committed the deed, so they decided not to report it. Chad said he would make sure that this would never happen again and that he was going over to talk to Katherine's parents.

When Chad arrived at Katherine's house he was hot, but his mood changed abruptly. Katherine's grandmother opened the door sobbing. Chad had known Katherine's grandmother for years and asked her what was wrong. She asked Chad to come in and sit down. She then told Chad that Katherine's parents received a phone call at 3 a.m. from the police. Katherine had been involved in a serious accident. She and two other girls swerved to miss a deer, lost control of their car and ran off the road into a tree. All three girls were alive, but just barely and Katherine was in the worst condition of the three. The news hit Chad very hard. He was angry with Katherine, but he didn't want anything bad to happen to her. After talking to her grandmother and getting all the information about which hospital she was in, he said a prayer with her and left.

Chad called Rachel from his cell phone to tell her the news and headed over to her house. Rachel was waiting for Chad outside and when he pulled up she rushed up to his car. She asked him if he was going to be okay. Chad told her that he was pretty shook up, but he thought he would be okay. Chad asked Rachel if she would be upset if he went to see Katherine. Rachel said not only did she not mind, but she insisted that he go and see her, and that she wanted to come too. Chad couldn't believe that after all the stuff Katherine had done to Rachel and her family, that she showed such love in return.

When Chad and Rachel arrived at the hospital, Rachel told Chad to go in and see Katherine alone. Rachel knew that even though

Chad was dating her now, he once loved Katherine and that he might want to talk to her privately. Rachel said she would wait for him in the lobby. Chad walked in and saw Katherine's parents first. Her mother had been given a pill to relax her nerves, and her father was holding Katherine's hand and crying. It was hard for Chad to see, because the girl he had once loved and who was always so beautiful now had bruises, scratches, and wounds all over her face and body. Chad tried to stay strong, but as he walked up to the bed where Katherine laid sleeping, tears filled his eyes and he began to weep. Just a few hours earlier Chad was ready to rip into Katherine about what she had done to Rachel's house. Now he was looking at her in a hospital bed. As Chad was crying, he knelt beside her bed and started praying for her to recover completely and quickly. While he prayed, he felt a hand touch his head. It was Katherine. She couldn't talk, but did manage a whisper. She told Chad that she was sorry for the way she had been acting and for what she did to Rachel. Then she told Chad how much she appreciated him being there, but he probably shouldn't have come because Rachel might not understand. Chad told Katherine not only did Rachel understand, but she insisted that he come, and she was waiting for him out in the lobby. That's when Katherine started to cry. How could Rachel be so different? How could she care about Katherine after all that she had done to her? Katherine asked Chad if he would go get Rachel and bring her to the room. Chad agreed and went to get her. Rachel walked in with a flower that she bought in the hospitals' gift shop. Katherine asked Rachel to come up to the bed so she could talk to her and not strain to speak. Katherine started crying all over again, and told Rachel she would understand if she hated her, and wouldn't forgive her, but she wanted to apologize anyway. If Rachel would agree, she would love to start over and be friends. Rachel said she had already forgiven her and as far as being friends, she thought the idea was a great one. Rachel then told Katherine that she should get some rest and that she would be praying for her to have a speedy recovery.

Katherine then surprised Chad and Rachel both by telling them she would be going to church with them as soon as she was out of the hospital. The couple said they would hold her to that promise and that they would see her again soon. Chad had always dreamed of the day that he would be able to share Christ's love with Katherine and she would actually be receptive, but he gave up on that idea after they broke up. Now it looked as if God was going to work it out, but not as Chad planned. Chad was thankful that Katherine's life was spared and that it looked like she and Rachel would be friends now. Unfortunately, it took something like almost losing her life to get through to her.

Chapter IX
The Record

Several weeks had passed since Katherine and her friends were in the accident and now all three girls were back in school. Katherine, true to her promise, started attending church with Chad and Rachel every time the doors were open, and not only that, but she and Rachel had become good friends.

Chad had been getting closer and closer to the all-time scoring record, and within the next game or two he would break it. Chad was looking forward to getting the record behind him. He was becoming weary of all the media crews and interviews before and after games. He just wanted to play basketball, and try to win a championship. Chad only needed 27 more points and he would stand alone as the most prolific scorer in state history. To be honest, the record didn't mean as much to Chad as it did before he got saved. Individual records were nice, but he now realized that he wouldn't have been able to accomplish it without all the teammates he played with over his four years, and winning a state title was a much greater achievement. Scoring titles can be taken away from you, but a state championship lives on forever, especially in the hearts of everyone who lives in Indiana.

Chad's team was unbeaten, and ranked first in the state polls, but on Friday they would face the second ranked team, who also was unbeaten. The team was from Jeffersonville, and featured not only one, but three kids who were committed to play Division I basketball after high school. Jeffersonville had always been a thorn in Chad's side. The two teams were in the same conference, and Jeffersonville had been one of the few teams that were able to shut him down in previous years.

Chad knew this would be his teams' toughest test to date. Not only was the Jeffersonville team loaded with talent, but the game was in their home gym, where they hadn't lost a game in five years. Before the game, while Chad and his team were warming up, the crowd started taunting them with the proverbial "Over-Rated" chant and, of course, there were others who used much stronger language. Chad just used that for fuel. As soon as the game started, Chad buried a three point shot. Jeffersonville answered right back with a three of their own. The whole first quarter the teams battled back and forth, and at the end of the quarter, the two teams were tied.

During the second quarter Chad was shut down, because he had to sit on the bench with three fouls. This gave Jeffersonville the opportunity to gain a 10 point advantage. This was the first time all year that Chad and his team had been losing at the half, and it didn't sit well with them.

In the third quarter they came out with a fury of baskets and by the end of the quarter, Chad's team was leading by 7 and Chad had 20 points. Chad had managed to go through the whole third quarter without picking up a fourth foul, and now his team had the lead. Chad felt confident that his team would pull off the victory and keep their record unblemished. But then, at the beginning of the fourth quarter, Chad got called on a touch foul, and had to retreat back to the bench. Chad couldn't do anything except watch as his team struggled without him to maintain its lead. They managed to survive through half of the quarter, but then Jeffersonville started a trapping full court press, and without Chad in the game, his team couldn't get the ball up the court. Jeffersonville took the lead with just three minutes to go. It was now time for Chad to go back in the game. As the seconds rolled off of the clock, Chad and his team trailed by 3 points. With just a few seconds left, Chad's coach called a timeout and set up a play for Chad to shoot a three point shot. Chad had made the shot many times and felt that this time shouldn't be any different. When Derrick passed the ball in to Chad, he took the shot as the buzzer sounded. It didn't go in, but there was a foul called. Chad would have to make three consecutive free throws just to make it to overtime. Chad had always been an excellent free throw shooter, and a clutch kind of guy. He had no doubt that this game, was going into overtime. Since Chad was fouled at the end of regulation, he would be the only player standing on the court. The Jeffersonville fans were all standing and yelling as Chad calmly took the ball and shot his first free throw. Nothing but net. One down, two to go. Chad going through the same routine as the first shot, put the second shot right through the middle as well. Now the fans were really getting loud, which made Chad focus that much more on his shot. As the referee gave the ball to Chad for his third and final shot, Chad dribbled three times, spun the ball backwards, got set, and let it fly. In and out! Chad and his team had lost their first game of the season, and Chad was the reason why. He couldn't believe he missed a free throw. Chad had only missed a handful of free throws all season, and now he missed the most important one of the year. The fans all stormed the court, and started chanting "we're number 1". Chad wanted to throw up, but he just walked to the locker room with his team.

  The ride home seemed to take forever because of the loss. Chad couldn't get out of his mind that he had cost his team a win by being in foul trouble, and by missing the free throw. When the team got back to their school, Chad went in the gym to shoot free throws. He shot 20 and hit 20, and then he went home.

  The next day was another day though, and Chad's team couldn't dwell on the loss of last night, they had another game to play tonight. This time they would play their county rival Mitchell. Chad had never lost a game to Mitchell, because they were a much smaller school. Mitchell always put up a good fight though, and he knew tonight would be no different. The best thing about this game was that it would be played at home, and Chad was only 5 points away from breaking the record.

When it came time for the doors to open to let people in for the game, the line was already so long that you couldn't see the front from the back. Not only that, but every news crew from around the state was there, waiting to catch the historical moment with their television cameras. Chad was feeling a little uneasy before the game, but then he said a little prayer, and asked God to help him play to the best of his abilities, and to keep everyone playing on both teams safe from injury. After that, Chad felt much better. Then he saw Rachel, who was smiling at him and mouthed I love you, which left him feeling completely at ease.

The game was a blowout from the start, Chad and his team won the game by 30 points and Chad scored 26. After the game, the school had scheduled a ceremony for Chad to honor him, and give him a chance to address the fans, and the media.

When Chad stepped up to the microphone, he got a five minute ovation. Chad was overwhelmed by the outpouring of love that he was being shown, and he had to fight back tears as he began to speak. Chad said that he first wanted to thank his Lord and Savior Jesus Christ, because without him, none of the good things in his life would be possible. Chad went on to say that he also wanted to thank his parents for all the time, money and support they had given him throughout the years. Chad said he would also like to thank Coach Bush for giving him the opportunity to play varsity basketball as a freshman, and for never losing faith in him. He also wanted to thank every teammate he played with each of his four years, because they always were the ones who gave him opportunities to score, and he couldn't have done it without them. Chad paused for a second and said that last but not least, he wanted to thank all the fans who had stuck with the team through good times and bad, and that he promised to make up for that free throw he missed down in Jeffersonville by bringing home a state title. The crowd erupted again for another long ovation. As it started to quiet down, a voice screamed out, "We love you Chad." Chad told the crowd that he loved all of them too. Then Chad said he couldn't leave without thanking two more people, Katherine and Rachel. Katherine was his girlfriend and best friend for the first three years of his career, and he wanted to thank her for being there for him then, and for being there for him still. Rachel, didn't have any idea of what she was getting herself in to when she started dating Chad, but she had never been anything but sweet, supportive, and a great example of how a Christian should act at all times. Chad told the crowd that he knew most people wouldn't understand how a girlfriend of three years and a new girlfriend could get along and have no feelings of jealousy, malice, or bitterness, but he knew it was the power of Christ in their lives. Chad ended his speech with a thank you and God bless you all. With the crowd standing and cheering, Chad walked off the court. Now with the record out of the way, Chad could focus on winning the state. There were just four games left before tournament play started, and Chad was ready.

Chapter X
The Sectional

The next four games were against teams that had little to no chance to beat them, so that gave Chad and his team a chance to rest up for the state tournament before it began. Chad and the other starters only played three quarters of each game, and the team still won by an average of 17 points.

When the draw for the Sectional came out, Chad and his team got one of the two coveted byes. Jeffersonville received the other. This meant in order for Chad to get another crack at Jeffersonville, they would both have to win one game, and then meet in the Sectional Final. Chad had been dreaming of playing them again, and getting his chance to redeem himself. First though, he would have to wait for the winner of the New Albany and Seymour game. Both teams were very good, and the Sectional was hosted by Seymour, which had only lost one game all year at home.

On the opening night of the Sectional, Chad and his team went to watch the game to see who they would be playing. It was a hard fought game, and both teams played very well. The lead changed back and forth between the two teams several times before Seymour, with one minute to play, finally pulled ahead for good. As the buzzer went off, Seymour had won the game by 7 points. Chad, and the rest of the team was hoping that New Albany could win, so that they could play on a neutral floor, instead of it being a home game for Seymour. Unfortunately it didn't work out that way. The only game Seymour had lost at home all year was to Jeffersonville, and that was only because they hit a half court shot at the buzzer. Chad's team had only beaten Seymour by four the first time they played, and that was at home. There was no doubt that the boys would have their work cut out for them on Friday night.

Coach Bush didn't like to have practices on Wednesday night because of church, but he called one for this Wednesday, and told everyone they needed to be there or else they would risk being benched. Chad didn't even consider missing church. He told Coach Bush he was sorry, but he wouldn't be able to make practice. Coach Bush told him he understood where Chad was coming from, but if he didn't come to practice, he would have to be benched. He couldn't make exceptions, even for him. Chad said he understood that, but it didn't change anything and he would see him at practice Thursday.

All day Wednesday at school the other boys on the team gave Chad a hard time about coming to practice. They told him that God wouldn't mind if he missed one time, and that if he didn't come and had to sit on the bench, they would probably lose. Chad told them that he was sorry, but his decision was final, and that they could win even if the coach benched him the whole game.

If Chad thought it was rough at school that day, it was even worse when he got home. Chad's dad was furious when he found out about Chad's intentions to miss practice. He demanded that Chad miss church and go to practice. He hadn't put in all that time, practice, and money all these years for Chad to throw it all away because he was trying to prove how religious he was now. Chad then informed his father that he wasn't trying to prove anything, he just felt like he needed to put God first. If that cost his team a chance at being champions, then so be it, but he knew that God wouldn't let him down. His dad wouldn't leave him alone about it until Chad told him if he didn't stop, he wasn't going to play in college next year. When his father heard that, he just stormed out of the room, and slammed the door.

Thankfully, Chad still had his church family, and of course Rachel, to talk things over with. After church that night, Chad went home and tried to talk to his dad, but he told him he had nothing to say. It hurt Chad that his dad couldn't understand, or even try to see things from his side, but he knew he was right in what he was doing. The next day Chad's teammates didn't even look at him. He tried to talk to them, but they just ignored him. After practice that night, Coach Bush asked Chad to stay so he could talk to him. Chad thought that it was going to be like his dad, and the other guys on the team, but when he got to the coaches' office, Coach Bush said something that surprised him. He told Chad that he was proud of him for sticking to his guns and that he gave the boys a vote at practice Wednesday night and they voted unanimously to let him play Friday. He still would have to start the game on the bench, but he would be allowed to play. Chad was ecstatic, and told the coach that he would do his best to help his team win. Coach Bush told Chad win or lose, he was proud of the young man that he had become, and that he knew he would never coach another kid like him.

The next day was Friday, and all day long Chad was thinking about the game. He knew that God was the reason that he was going to be able to play, and he was going to make the best of it. The boys on the team were still mad, but he knew they would get over it, especially when the game was coming down the wire, and they needed him. After school, Chad got home and found balloons, flowers and a card waiting for him. They were from Rachel, and the card said that she admired and loved him, and promised that she would be there cheering him on. Chad always loved to see Rachel at games. If things weren't going well, or the other fans were getting on him, he could just look up at Rachel and she would smile. That always made everything else go away.

When it came time for the bus to leave for Seymour, nobody

would talk to Chad, or wanted to sit with him, except for one, Katherine. Katherine asked Chad if the seat next to him was taken, and asked him if he remembered the last time that happened. They both laughed and Chad said yes, but this time he was happy she was there to take the seat. Now that Katherine was going to church, and friends with Rachel, it was a whole new ballgame.

Finally the bus arrived at the gym, and the team went to the locker room. After the boys got dressed, Coach Bush gave the team their instructions for the game, and a speech. He told the boys that they had been the best team he had ever coached, but if they lost tonight, everything they had achieved up to this point wouldn't matter. The only way they could end the season properly, was with a State Title, and that was just exactly what he planned on doing. With that said the boys all huddled up, gave a cheer, and went out on the court to warm up.

As the buzzer sounded, indicating that it was time to start the game, anxiety started to rise in Chad. He had never started a game on the bench before, and he didn't know how it would affect his game. He didn't like the thought of entering a game cold without having a good sweat, but he didn't regret his decision and knew he could adjust. From the opening tip, Seymour took control of the game, scoring on their first five possessions. Chad sat patiently on the bench, and cheered his teammates on, but inside it was killing him. He knew that if he didn't get in the game soon, that his team may not be able to come back. After the first quarter, Chad and his team were trailing Seymour by 14 points.

Mr. Bush told Chad it was time for him to get in there and be the player everyone thought him to be. Chad jumped up and ran to the scorers table to check in. Seymour had the ball to start the second quarter, and as soon as they threw it in, Chad stole the ball and took it in for a dunk. Half of the gym erupted with cheers, while the other half groaned, but one thing was for sure, everyone knew that number 5 was in the game and ready to play.

By the time the second quarter came to an end, Chad and his team had cut the lead to 7 points. When the team came out to start the third quarter, Chad felt great, and knew in his heart that his team would come back and win the game. Seymour had other plans though, and after the third quarter, they increased their lead to 10. Chad's faith didn't waver though, and he encouraged his team to reach down inside and play with everything they had.

To start the fourth, Chad hit big shot after big shot, and his team cut the lead to 4 with a minute to go. Seymour started to run the four corner offense, in order to get fouled or run the clock out. Chad and his team fouled quickly so they could make the game last longer, and make Seymour earn points from the free throw line. As the last minute came to a close, Seymour still had a 2 point lead with just 9 seconds remaining.

Mr. Bush called a time-out to set up a final play. He knew that Seymour would be keying on Chad for the final shot, so he drew up a play for Derrick. Derrick had come up big for the team many times and had all the confidence in the world in his own abilities. Chad, being the decoy, took the ball and dribbled it up the floor. With 4 seconds he passed the ball to Derrick for the shot, and then went to the basket to rebound in case of a miss. The ball hit the rim and bounced off. Just when it looked like all was lost, Chad came flying in and slammed the missed shot home, and was fouled on the play to boot. Once again everyone started going crazy. Seymour's entire crowd wanted a foul on Chad for going over the back, and all of the fans of Chad's team were cheering and talking about what an awesome play it was. No matter which opinion the crowd had, the fact was the game was now tied, and Chad was shooting a free throw with only one second left to potentially win the game. Immediately Chad's mind went back to the Jeffersonville game, and how he didn't come through that night. He was sure tonight would be different.

Seymour's coach called a time-out to try to ice Chad, but that didn't bother him. All the Seymour fans were screaming and waving their hands back and forth from the stands behind the basket, but that didn't bother him either. Chad was calm and cool as he stepped up to the line for his free throw. He went through the same routine that he had been doing since he started playing as a kid, and let it go. Swish…Right through the center. Now all Chad's team had to do was not let Seymour catch the ball and hit a shot during that last second. Coach Bush called a time-out and set up the defense. When the referee handed the Seymour player the ball, he threw it all the way to the other end of the court, where Chad stole the ball to end the game. Chad and his team had come back and beat a solid team on their home court.

Now the only team standing in their way of advancing to the Regional was Jeffersonville, who had already won their game easily. Chad was looking forward to playing the team who hung the lone loss on his record. He knew it would be a war, but he was up for the chance at evening the score, only this time, it was win or your season is over. Chad went home and tried to sleep, but he struggled. He couldn't wait to get back on the court. On Saturday morning, the team met for breakfast, and then went to the school to go over film and game strategy with the coach. After meeting Rachel for lunch Chad had to go back to school to ride the team bus back to Seymour. This time everyone was talking to Chad just as if nothing ever happened. Chad didn't hold it against them that they treated him so poorly the past few days. He just wanted them to get along and work together as a team.

Right before the game started, Chad said a prayer. He told God that most of all he wanted everyone to be protected on both teams, and that win or lose, he wanted to have the right kind of attitude when it was over. After his prayer, it was time to start the game.

Jeffersonville got the opening tip and proceeded right down the floor for a basket. The Jeff fans were rowdy as ever, and every time Chad touched the ball they would start to yell and taunt him about the free throw he missed the last time they played. It was a well played game throughout, but Chad and his team were on a mission and by the half, Chad's team had the lead.

The third quarter got underway with a bang. Jeffersonville threw a lob pass to one of their big men for a rim rattling dunk, which brought their fans alive. Chad and his team tried to counter with a similar play for him, but it was stolen and taken down the court for another dunk. Coach Bush called time, and tried to settle the boys down, but he knew this game was definitely going to have a close finish. At the end of the third, the score was tied.

The fourth quarter was nip and tuck, and Chad was being shut down by Jeffersonville's stifling defense. Every time he touched the ball, he had two or three guys surround him. Derrick, on the other hand, was having a great game and when Chad would get double and triple teamed, he would kick it out to Derrick for the shot.

With under a minute left, Chad's team was ahead by 2 points and had the ball. Jeffersonville would try to steal the ball with their pressure defense, but if they couldn't get a steal, they would have to foul. Jeffersonville came close to stealing the ball a few times, but they could only manage to force a time-out or knock the ball out of bounds. As the clock rolled down to ten seconds showing, they needed to put someone on the line. Chad was the best free throw shooter on the team, so the ball was in his hands when Jeffersonville committed the foul.

As Chad stepped up to take his shots, the Jeff crowd started chanting "Just like last time." Chad didn't let it faze him and calmly put the first shot up and through the center, not even touching any rim. That pushed the lead to 3 points, with one more shot to make it 4. Chad again eyed the rim and the sea or Jeffersonville fans sitting behind the goal. Again Chad put it right down the middle.

Jeffersonville quickly drove the length of the floor and scored a basket to cut the lead back down to 2 points with five seconds remaining. After the basket, Jeffersonville called its last time-out.

Coach Bush set up the play for Chad to get the ball again, but this time the play didn't work, and they had to inbound it to Derrick. Derrick was knocked to the floor as soon as he touched it and now could put the game out of reach by making a pair of free throws. Derrick stepped up and did just that, he made them both.

Now all Chad's team had to do was not foul and let the clock run out. Jeffersonville came down the floor and hit a three point shot at the buzzer, but the game was over, and Chad's team had won by the slimmest of margins, 1 point. After the game, all the reporters who were there to cover the big game, wanted to talk to Chad, but he told them they needed to talk to Derrick, because he was the hero with the way he kept them in the game during the fourth quarter, and by making the two biggest free throws of the season. Chad was just happy to get out of Seymour with a Sectional Championship, and was now looking forward to playing in the Regional.

After the game in the locker room, Derrick went to Chad and told him thanks for giving him the credit, and sending the reporters over. Chad told Derrick he deserved it, he played an awesome game. Derrick then asked Chad if he would like to come to the party he was going to have that night. Chad told him thanks, but he didn't feel comfortable around that scene anymore. Derrick said he knew and understood, but he still wanted to invite him as a token of friendship. Chad appreciated the offer, but he had plans to spend time with Rachel. Chad told Derrick to be careful, and try not to overdo it too much. Derrick just laughed and said he would be good. They both knew he wouldn't be.

Chapter XI
The Semi State

The night of Derricks' party, he and one of his friends from the football team got arrested for drinking. He didn't have to spend the night in jail, but because he was arrested, Indiana high school rules for athletes, demand that a player must sit out a minimum of two games. This meant that Derrick wouldn't be eligible to play in the upcoming Regional game, or the first game of the Semi State.

This was a tremendous loss for the team. Derrick was the second leading scorer on the team, and was an outstanding defender as well. The team who they would be meeting in the Regional wasn't a threat, because the Regional was played at home and the team they would play came from a weak Sectional. That would be different when they got to the Semi State. There would most likely be two ranked teams waiting for them, because the Semi State is the last sixteen teams left in the tournament.

Derrick felt horrible and apologized to the team, but most of the boys just told him that he was stupid, and if they lost, it would be his fault. Chad was extremely angry at first and felt the same way the other boys did, but then he realized that Derrick didn't mean to hurt the team, and that he just made a mistake. Chad went to Derrick and told him not to worry, because they were going to win the two games he had to sit out, and that they would all be able to win the state together. Fighting back tears, Derrick thanked Chad for being cool about everything, and apologized again for hurting the team. Chad just laughed, and told Derrick he was glad he had to miss two games, because now he could score more and get the publicity back he lost to

Derrick at the Sectional. Derrick laughed and told Chad that he better score all he could while he sat out, because when he could play he was going to take over again.

Chad was happy that he could get Derrick to joke around with him. Chad knew how much it meant to Derrick to win the state, and how hard it would be for him to sit and watch while the team played without him. What Chad thought about most though, was if he had not been a Christian, he would have been there with Derrick, drinking, and would be made to sit out too. Thankfully for Chad, and the team, that was not the case.

On the night of Regional Derrick was hurting, but he was nothing but supportive of the team, and his replacement. The whole game he cheered, clapped, and got everyone on the bench pumped up. As expected, the score wasn't close, even without Derrick playing. The team won the game by 20 points and now it was on to the Semi State.

Chad's team, because of where they were located in the state, had to play in the Indianapolis Semi State. Not only did they have to play in Indianapolis, but the teams they would be up against were from Bloomington, and Indianapolis. The kids from those teams were usually very big, athletic and talented. Every team had at least one kid going to a division 1 school, and several other kids going to smaller schools to play. Without Derrick, it would be almost impossible to win, but Chad knew that no matter what, he was going to give it his best shot. If they could somehow win the first game, he would have Derrick back, and then he was sure it would be on to state.

All week at practice Coach Bush worked on doing something his team had never done before, and that was to play a zone defense. He knew that the other team wouldn't be expecting it, and he also knew without Derrick, they couldn't play man to man because they didn't match up well. He worked on several different versions of the zone and the boys learned each one quickly. When it was time for the boys to play, the coach told them to start in man to man defense, because he wanted to surprise them with the zones in the second half.

During the first quarter, Chad struggled to get shots. Every time he touched the ball, the other team double teamed him. He was getting frustrated, but he knew it was a long game and that he had to stay in the game mentally. After the first quarter his team was trailing by 7 points.

As the second quarter got under way, Chad broke free for some shots, and brought his team to within 2 points by half. Since the team was only down two at half, the coach decided to continue playing man to man until the fourth. Derrick was still being the number one cheerleader for his team throughout the game. He got water and towels for his teammates coming out of the game, and always encouraged them to keep playing hard. It was hard for him not to be out there, but he knew if they could just win this game he would have his shot to redeem himself.

When the third quarter ended, Chad and his team were tied with the powerhouse team from Indy. Now it was time to spring the trap on them and start the zone. Coach Bush knew that the Indy team was big, athletic, and talented, but he also knew that they didn't really have any kids who could shoot from the three point line. He instructed his team to pack the zone in, and make them shoot jumpers from the perimeter. Chad's team had the ball to start the quarter, and quickly scored on a set play. Then the boys went to the other side, and set up in a one-three-one zone. The coach for the other team quickly called a time-out, and set up their zone offense. Coach Bush took advantage of the time-out to instruct his team to get in one of the other zone defenses they worked on at practice. When the Indy team came back on the floor, Chad and his team set up in a one-two-two zone.

The Indy team looked lost and quickly turned the ball over for a break away dunk by Chad. This gave his team a 4 point advantage.

Again, the Indy team tried to solve the zone, but could not. They tried to force it inside, but just turned the ball over again. This time Chad found Derricks' replacement for a break away lay-up. For the rest of the game the team from Indianapolis tried to find a way to score the ball, but nothing they did seemed to work. As the final seconds ticked off the clock, Chad and his team had pulled ahead by 10 and had pulled off a miraculous victory.

The first person Chad went to was Derrick and told him he guessed he wouldn't mind sharing the ball and the limelight a little. Derrick laughed, and told Chad he could have anything he wanted, he was just happy he would be able to play again.

Derrick would have his chance that night. Unlike Sectional, and Regional, Semi State was played in one day. Two semi-final games in the morning and the championship game that night. After their game, Chad's team stayed and watched the next game to see who they would play. It was a tremendous game between two ranked teams. As the game ended, the team from Bloomington went ahead for good. This meant Chad would go up against his old nemesis Greg Gordon. Chad knew whoever won this game would be the frontrunner for Mr. Basketball, and the favorite to win the State.

Coach Bush told the kids they could leave with their family, or friends, but to be back by 5 p.m., and to stay out of trouble until then. Chad and Rachel went to eat and to look around at the giant mall downtown. Chad tried to have fun, and not dwell on the game, but it was hard for him not to. He knew how much Greg and his team would like to revenge their only loss of the year, and put Chad's team out of the tourney. Rachel could tell Chad was stressed out and as always, she knew just what to do and say to help him relax.

When it came time to head back to the arena, instead of feeling stressed out, or anxious, Chad was now feeling excited. He was now one game away from making it to the State Finals, and three wins away from being a champion. First, he and his team had to win tonight's game, and that wasn't going to be easy.

After the teams left the locker rooms and warmed up, it was time to start the game. It wasn't a good start for Chad. He missed his first five shots and even air-balled one, and at the end of the first quarter his team found itself down by half a dozen. Chad had no idea why he started so poorly, but he knew if he didn't get the problem fixed soon, his team would be going home for good.

Then in the second quarter, Derrick started hitting every shot he threw up, and single handedly put the team ahead by 3 points at the half. Through two quarters, Chad only had 7 points. He hadn't scored under 20 all year, and now it didn't look like he would even come close to that.

During halftime Coach Bush told Chad that he thought he was pressing too much, and to just relax, and let the game come to him. It proved to be sound advice, and in the third quarter Chad exploded for 12 points and his team now had a lead of 15.

Just when it looked like Greg and his team was down for the count, they came roaring back with a furious pressing defense and cut the lead down to five with two minutes to play. It was with a minute left that Derrick fouled out, trying to block a shot. Not only did he foul out, but the kid made the shot and the free throw, tying the game. Chad and Derrick had been scoring most of the points in the second half, but now Derrick was out of the game, and Chad was being double teamed.

As the clock expired, Chad's team was holding the ball for the last shot, but with ten seconds left, Greg stole the ball and started down the court for a dunk, but Chad caught and fouled him before he could get to the basket. This meant that Greg had a chance to make a pair of free throws. Greg was an excellent free throw shooter and had already made 9 free throws in 9 attempts. He put the first one up and through, not even touching the rim. Then Coach Bush called a time-out trying to ice Greg, and also to set up a play in case he hit the free throw, and one if he missed it.

When Greg got the ball, he aimed and fired, but he left it short. Chad snatched the rebound and pushed it up the floor. He was trying to take it coast to coast, but as he went up to shoot, Greg blocked his shot out of bounds. Now there was just a few seconds left, and Chad's team had to inbound the ball from under the basket. Coach Bush called his final time-out and drew up a play for Chad to be a decoy. He knew that all eyes would be on Chad to take the shot, so he had two players set a double screen for Chad. They would fake the pass to Chad, and then the top guy who screened for Chad would sprint down to the front of the basket for a lay-up.

As the boys set up, the coach screamed at the screener to get the pick set for Chad, in order to throw the other team off. When the referee blew his whistle, Chad took off for the double screen just as he was instructed, and yelled for the ball. It worked like a charm. Almost the whole Bloomington team followed Chad and left the top guy wide open, as he sprinted under the basket for a lay-up. Chad and his team had finally done it. They were going to play for a State Championship.

After the basket, all the Bloomington kids dropped to their knees in agony from defeat. They had played their guts out, and came up a basket short of winning.

Chad went over to Greg and told him he played a great game, but Greg couldn't get over the fact that he missed a free throw. Chad knew what it felt like to miss a free throw in a big situation and tried to console him, but to no avail. Before Chad left, Greg told him that he better win the State, because if he had to lose, he wanted the team who beat him to be the champions. Chad thanked him and told him he would try his hardest to bring it home for the both of them. Chad actually felt bad for Greg, but he was thankful that his team survived to play another day. Now he just had to win two more games and he would be a State Champion.

Chapter XII
The State

All the way home from Indianapolis, the boys laughed and celebrated being the Semi State Champions. Chad's dream of being a State Champion was now within his grasp. They had already beaten the teams that were supposed to be his teams' main competition, they survived two games without Derrick and now he was back and playing better than ever. Chad knew he couldn't overlook any opponent, but he definitely liked his teams' chances.

When the team pulled into the school parking lot, there was a crowd of people waiting on them to show their appreciation for the accomplishment of making it to the State Finals. As the boys were getting off of the bus the crowd burst into simultaneous cheers and applause. None of the boys expected anyone to be waiting on them, but when they saw and heard the crowd cheering it made them feel like heroes.

The next day was Sunday, and for Chad that meant going to church. Church was usually the last place he ever expected to hear or talk about basketball, but when he walked in, that's all anyone talked about to him.

After the service Chad spent the day with Rachel. The only downside about his team still playing in the tournament was that it was taking up most of his time, and leaving very little time to see Rachel.

Coach Bush had been practicing the boys every night after school, except on Wednesday, because of what happened last time. That meant Chad would wake up, go to school, stay after for practice and then go home just in time to do homework. When he finished his homework, he could call Rachel but by that time it was late and Rachel had a phone curfew. Rachel's parents graciously extended the curfew by half an hour. They were happy to receive that but it still left very little time to talk.

Chad was happy that there would only be one more week of this crazy schedule. All week long both the school and town were in a buzz over the upcoming games. The printing classes made posters and tee shirts. The faculty, students and staff wore the shirts supporting the team, and the town shops hung banners and painted their windows wishing them good luck.

The team would be leaving for Indianapolis on Friday after school. They were going to practice on Friday night at the arena and then spend the night at a hotel nearby.

The first team they would have to try to defeat was Marion. Marion had been a very successful program in years past, with multiple championships, but this was their first trip back to the finals in several years.

If Chad's team could win their first game they would play the winner of the Gary Roosevelt and Valparaiso game. Gary was always a team filled with remarkable athletes, and this year was no exception. Valparaiso was lead by two players who were each six feet, nine inches tall, and were signed to play college basketball for the college rival of Chad's college choice. Chad's week seemed to drag on and on, but finally Friday came and the team left for Indianapolis.

The State Championship was usually held at the arena where the pro basketball team played, but this year it was moved to the huge dome where the pro football team played. The move was made because of all of the hoop-la and fan-fair surrounding Chad and the two boys from Valparaiso. Playing in front of a huge crowd was nothing new to the boys, but this would be extremely different from anything the state had ever seen up to this point in time. No other high school game in history would be played in front of as many people as this game. The staggering amount of tickets sold to watch this event was 43,755.

As the boys arrived for their practice they found that the shooting background took a lot of getting use to. The dome was so large and open that it played tricks with their depth perception. It even gave Chad trouble. After the team finished up practice they showered, got dressed, ate dinner together and headed to the hotel.

Chad was assigned to a room with Derrick because Coach Bush knew Chad was the only one who could keep him out of trouble for the night. Due to their nerves and excitement, the two boys had trouble trying to fall asleep that night. Chad was trying to pray as he laid in his bed, but Derrick kept asking him question after question. Derrick had always tried to come across as someone who never had any fear, but tonight he was afraid. He was worried that he wouldn't play well and that he would let the team down. Chad assured him that he would be fine and that the only way he would play bad was if he was too tired from staying up all night asking these crazy questions. Derrick laughed and then he did something that caught Chad by surprise. He asked Chad if he would say a prayer for him. Chad told Derrick that he already prayed for him every night, but he promised he would throw in an extra one for him so he could get some rest. That was the last thing said between the boys that night. Before Chad went to sleep, he thanked God that Derrick had taken a step in the right direction and that he allowed them to be in the same room. Chad knew that Derrick wouldn't have asked anyone else to pray for him, or even talk about God to anyone else on the team except him, so he knew it was the Lords' will for them to be placed together that night.

The next morning the team ate breakfast and headed to the dome. After pre-game warm-ups, the team went to the locker room for some last minute preparations and strategy. Coach Bush told the boys they still had a lot of unfinished business to take care of, and if they wanted to be victorious, everyone would have to do their part. The boys were then given their defensive assignments for the game and headed out to the court. With the sound of the buzzer, it was time for the tip off.

Marion won the tip, and took the ball straight to the basket for 2 points. Before Chad's team could get the ball thrown in, Marion caught them off guard with a great man to man press, which produced a steal and a basket, pushing the score to 4 points to zero.

Coach Bush was forced to call a time-out to settle the team down and set up the press breaker. Coming out of the time-out, Chad and the boys started playing inspired basketball and quickly tied the game. From that point on, it was a dog fight and at the end of the quarter Marion had the lead by 1 point.

Up to this point in the game, Chad had not been able to do much, because Marion was concentrating most of their defensive attention towards him. Derrick on the other hand had been playing like a man possessed. At the beginning of the second quarter, the coach set up a play for Chad, which resulted in a slam dunk. Chad was hoping that the dunk would get him started, but unfortunately he could only manage to get one more basket before half. The teams were tied at half and Chad was held to 7 points. Derrick was the one who was keeping the team in the game with his 14 points and 8 rebounds.

As the third quarter started, Chad was still being held in check by his defender. Chad tried everything he knew to do to get open and shake the guy off of him, but nothing he did worked and by the end of the quarter Chad and the boys were trailing Marion by 5 points.

Chad was starting to feel discouraged because he felt like he was letting everyone down with his poor play, but then, in the fourth quarter, something happened that changed the whole complexion of the game. The player who had been doing such a phenomenal job of defending him started talking trash to him. He informed Chad that he was about the easiest person he had guarded all year, including his little sister and that he didn't know had Chad got a scholarship to play basketball, unless he was going to play for the girls team. He then said he didn't think Chad was good enough to play for them either.

That was just the fuel Chad needed to get his game back. Chad started hitting every shot he took. He connected on four straight from behind the three point line even with the defender right in his face. The boy quickly shut up, but it was too late. Chad was already in the zone. With a minute left to play, Chad's team was now ahead by 4 points and Marion had the ball. The Marion coach screamed out a play from the sideline, which his team ran, and connected on a long three pointer cutting the lead to 1 point.

Marion's coach quickly called a time-out to go over who to foul in case they couldn't get a quick steal. Coach Bush used the time-out to set up a play to get Chad the ball. Chad got the ball, and waited to get fouled, but Marion didn't foul. Instead they trapped Chad and forced a turnover resulting in a dunk and Marion's lead with only 3 seconds left on the clock.

Coach Bush called his last time-out to set up some kind of miracle play. The Marion coach told his team not to press because he didn't want anyone to get a foul called on them and with only a few seconds left, he knew that Chad's team had to hope for a desperation shot to win.

As Coach Bush was giving his team their instructions, Chad sat there bewildered. Chad had never felt so down before in his life. He couldn't believe that he of all people turned the ball over and cost his team the chance to be champions. Chad couldn't make sense of it, but as he walked out on the court, possibly for the last time in his high school career, he said a prayer and told the Lord that he was thankful that he had been given the opportunity to make it this far, and that he wanted Gods' will to be done and not his own.

When the ref handed Derrick the ball to inbound, he riffled a pass to Chad near half court. Chad took two dribbles and took the shot. The shot hung in the air for what seemed like eternity, but it came down and when it did, it went right through the center of the basket. Chad had done it! The mistake he made just seconds before had been erased by a buzzer beater near mid-court. His teammates mobbed him where he stood and the Marion kids sunk to the floor.

It was the best game Chad had ever had the privilege of being apart of and he was thankful his team came out on top. Chad, struggling to get up from the bottom of the pile of his teammates, got up and made his way over to the player on Marion's team who had shut him down for three quarters and told him he was by far the best defender he had faced all year and that he played an awesome game. The boy thanked him for the compliment and told him he didn't mean any of the things he said during the game and that he was only doing it to get in his head. Chad didn't tell him that the trash talk was what made him play better, but a little part of the old Chad wanted to.

After all the handshakes and well wishes by the two teams, they went to their locker rooms. After Coach Bush made an end of speaking, the boys showered and went back out to the court to watch the next game. Most of the boys didn't care who won the game. They just hoped that whoever they played had to play a long, hard game and would be as tired as they were when they met in the final. Chad on the other hand was for Valparaiso. He really wanted a shot at the two guys going to the rival school. Valparaiso made Chad happy but not the rest of his team. They came out and took care of business against the overmatched Gary Roosevelt team. Valparaiso led the whole game, and never looked back, winning by 20 points. Now Chad was just one game away from what he believed to be his destiny.

After watching Valparaiso destroy Gary, Chad and his team headed to the local mall to look around and grab something to eat. Coach Bush made sure they all stayed together, because there is safety in numbers and he liked his teams to do everything together to create unity.

When it was finally time for the boys to head back to the dome, Chad started feeling butterflies about the game. After everyone got their uniforms on, Coach Bush came in to talk to the boys. Coach Bush said he was done preaching to them, because by this time they should all know what was expected of them. He also said that he wasn't going to give them the speech about how they've come too far to let it slip through their hands now. What he did say was that he wanted everyone to remember the looks on the faces of the Marion kids after the game. Coach Bush wanted them to remember because if they didn't come out ready to play, they would be the ones down on their hands and knees crying. To get this far only to lose was worse than getting put out in the first game of the Sectional. Then he asked the boys if any of them remembered who won the State five years ago. All of the boys raised their hands. Then he asked if any of them remembered who they beat. None of them raised their hand this time. Coach Bush informed them that the team that lost the game that night was the number one ranked team in the state at the time, just like they were and that the only game they lost all year was by 2 points in the State Final. The point that he was making was this - no matter how great of a season you have up to that point, people only remember champions. Coach Bush then huddled his team up and told them he was proud of them and that he was confident that if they played as hard as they could, and gave it their all, at the end of the night they would be champions. The boys were fired up after the speech and stormed out of the locker room and onto the court.

The dome was filled with a buzz, and electricity filled the air. Every newspaper and news media crew from the state was there to cover the game, as were several national crews. After all, Chad was ranked the number one prep basketball player in the country and the two kids from Valparaiso were also highly touted prep stars.

Right before the game started the referees had the captains from each team meet at half court and go over what was expected of them in terms of sportsmanship and fair play. Chad and Derrick were the representatives for their team and, of course, the two stand out players represented Valparaiso. Everyone shook hands after the briefing from the referees and then went back to their respective teams. As the buzzer sounded to start the game, the boys got some last minute instructions from the coaching staff and took the floor.

When the referee tossed the ball into the air to start the game, light bulb flashes filled the dome. Chad's team controlled the tip, and set up their offense. All year long Valparaiso had been living off of the turnovers they caused with their defense. The two big men seemed to block every shot or get every rebound, which allowed their guards to get out and run the open court for easy transition lay-ups. Chad and his team knew if they didn't take good shots, take care of the ball or get back on defense, they could be blown out quickly.

Throughout the first quarter Chad's team did all of the things they needed to do, but Valparaiso was playing excellent too. At the end of the quarter, each team had a total of 15 points. The coaching staff was happy with the effort of the boys in the first quarter, but they told the boys that for the rest of the game they just wanted them to win the quarter.

God, Life and Basketball

At the beginning of the second quarter Valparaiso switched defenses and started playing a box and one, which meant four guys played a zone defense and the other guy's job was to chase Chad everywhere he went. The defense worked like a charm for a short time, but then Coach Bush called a time-out and made the proper adjustment. Chad was now to run the point, which meant he was to distribute the ball to the other players on his team and create opportunities for them to score.

Derrick would now be the team's focal point on offense. Coach Bush had Derrick set up in the corner as Chad would drive the ball to the basket which made the zone collapse, leaving Derrick open to knock down jump shots. It proved to be a brilliant move because Derrick once again caught fire with his shooting and knocked down shot after shot, forcing Valparaiso back to man to man defense. For the rest of the quarter the two teams played evenly, but at the half Chad's team had a 5 point cushion.

During halftime Coach Bush encouraged the boys to keep up the good work and to go out and win the next quarter like they did the previous one. He also told everyone to work together to find their big guys and block them out. The big men from Valparaiso were doing what they did best and that was grabbing every rebound on both sides of the court. Coach Bush knew his team had to battle them on the boards or they wouldn't win.

In the third quarter the boys did a much better job of blocking out and Chad showed why he was the consensus number one ranked player in the country, scorching the nets for 15 points and giving his team a 12 point lead. After their strong play in the third quarter, the boys started feeling like the game was over and they started celebrating in the huddle. Coach Bush, being a veteran of many years, tried to make the boys understand that the game was far from over and if they stopped playing hard now, they would lose the game. Coach Bush told the boys that having the big lead was better than being behind, but Valparaiso was too good of a team to roll over for them Valparaiso hadn't been able to make it this far by not being fighters. He went on to say that if he knew anything at all about basketball he could promise them that Valparaiso, like any good champion with their backs against the wall, would come out swinging in the fourth quarter.

Valparaiso made Coach Bush look like a prophet at the start of the final quarter. The Valparaiso team came out with a renewed fire and intensity that knocked Chad and his team back on their heels. Every player on Valparaiso started diving for loose balls, getting a hand in every shooters face and fighting for every rebound. The two big men started throwing their muscle around, scoring at will around the basket, and blocking shot after shot. Midway through the quarter the lead had evaporated and now Chad's team only possessed a 4 point lead.

At this point, Coach Bush called a time-out and got in his players faces. He had warned them about what would happen if they stopped playing hard, and now they were in danger of losing the game and losing their chance to be champions. Coach Bush told the boys that he couldn't do anything else for them and that they could either go out and play hard to win, or they could keep playing the way they were and be forgotten in five years.

The message hit home, and the boys answered the call. From that point on they played with the same tenacity they had in the previous three quarters. They built their lead back up to 8 points, but Valparaiso kept battling too and would answer with spurts of their own to keep the game close.

As the game came down to the last minute, Chad and his team was holding on to a 6 point lead and had the ball. Valparaiso was forced to foul, and Chad had the ball. He calmly stepped up to the line and pushed the lead back to 8. Valparaiso quickly pushed the ball up the court and sank a big three point shot to cut the lead back to 5. This time Derrick was the recipient of the foul, but he could only make one of the two free throws. With the lead now at 6 points, Valparaiso once again pushed the ball up the floor, but this time they found one of their big men open under the basket for a dunk and a free throw opportunity, because he was fouled. The big man made good on his free throw, cutting the lead to 3 points with 30 seconds to go. Chad's team got the ball to him this time and he again made both free throws, extending the lead back to 5.

Valparaiso, being out of time-outs, had to hurry. They hit their best outside shooter for a long bomb, but his shot was off the mark and Derrick collected the rebound. He found Chad, who had broken free from the pack and threw down a monstrous slam dunk.

With the lead now at 7 and 5 seconds left on the clock, the game was in hand. As the final seconds rolled off the clock and the buzzer sounded, Chad's team had done it! They were State Champions!! Chad was overcome with joy and he ran off the court, past the security guards, into the stands and into the arms of his parents and Rachel.

Chad had finally seen his dream of being a State Champion come to pass. The only thing missing was that Jordan wasn't there to share it with him, but he knew Jordan was watching from Heaven and celebrating with him there.

After the teams left the floor, Chad was summoned to the green room to answer questions from the media. Chad had been given the MVP award for being the most outstanding player in the tournament. He had averaged over 21 points a game for the tournament and finished with 26 in the championship.

Chad accepted the honor with humility and wore the medal as he answered questions. After answering questions for about twenty minutes, he told the media that he would like to go celebrate with his teammates and excused himself. Chad was still in ecstasy over the feeling it gave him to have finally won the State. Chad wasn't sure if his team would ever make it, but now that they did he was extremely thankful. Chad knew that if it wasn't for the strength he gained from the Lord he wouldn't have been able to realize his dream. He knew he wouldn't have been able to get past Jordan's death. Chad realized that he would have been with Derrick the night he got arrested for drinking, which meant both he and Derrick would have had to sit out and his team would have had zero chance of advancing. Chad knew God had been the reason for all of his success and he was sure to let everyone know that whenever he spoke to them about it.

    Chad went on to achieve all of his goals for that year. He won the coveted Mr. Basketball award for the state, he was an Indiana All Star, along with being named to every All American team nationally and to top it all off, he was given the honor of being named the best player in the country.

    At every ceremony, awards banquet or anytime he was given an opportunity to address an audience, he remembered to always thank Jesus Christ for making it all happen. Chad knew that without him he would have never been anything more than a lowly sinner, sentenced to death and Hell. Chad also knew that without the Lord, he would have never met Rachel nor would he have seen Katherine get saved. Even his old party buddy Derrick started going with him to church and it looks like now he will be starting a relationship with Jesus too. All of this happened because Jordan never gave up on his friend and finally got him to church camp. How many people would be saved if someone would just tell them about Jesus and his love and invite them to church?

The End.

STUDY GUIDE

CHAPTER I
The Beginning

Chad Palmer was a very popular person in his school and in his community.

- What does it take to be popular today? What attributes, attitudes and abilities make you popular?

Although Chad seemed to have everything he could ever hope for at this point in his life, Jordan realized that the most important thing was missing in his friend's life – A personal relationship with Jesus Christ.

- Read and Discuss Matthew 16:24-28

- What makes if difficult to witness to a friend, especially a friend who seems to have everything the world has to offer?

- Read and Discuss II Timothy 1:7-9

Jordan was persistent in his efforts to witness to his friend. The message of the camp pastor touched Chad's heart, and after learning about what Jesus went through to bring us salvation, Chad gave his heart to Christ.

- Read and Discuss Philippians 2:1-8

- What did Jesus give up and go through in order to be born and become our Savior?

- Why would this message possibly lead others to become a Christian?

Although Chad, Jordan and his friends at church camp rejoiced in his decision to become a follower of Jesus Christ, not every shared in that excitement.

- Read and Discuss I Peter 4:1-6

- What is it about becoming a Christian that old friends might not like, or might resent?

PRAYER
Ask God to reveal to you a person to whom you can witness and then pray for the courage to do so.

CHAPTER II
Changes

Upon leaving church camp, Chad was experiencing spiritual elation. Now at home, he begins to face temptations and challenges to his faith.

- Identify and discuss the three temptations Chad had to face immediately upon coming home:

    1. Sexual (with Katherine)
        How important is your Christian faith when choosing a boyfriend or girlfriend?

    2. Social (with his friends)
        How important is your Christian faith when choosing your friends?

    3. Discouragement (with his family)
        What makes it difficult if you have a family that does not share your faith?

- Read and Discuss Matthew 4:1-11

    Before beginning his ministry, Jesus was faced with three temptations. What were they and how did Jesus overcome them?

PRAYER:
Share with God the things that tempt you the most and ask for His strength to overcome these temptations.

CHAPTER III
Back To School

Chad had a lot of decisions to make concerning his future. He had a lot of people awaiting his decisions.

- What are some of your plans and goals for life?

- Read and Discuss Matthew 6:25-33

    There are so many things to think about when planning ahead for your life. How do these words of Jesus encourage you?

As Chad considered God's will for his life, and what he wanted to do with his life, he took certain steps toward making a decision.

- What steps did Chad take?

- Who do you tend to go to for advice and guidance? Why?

PRAYER:
Ask God to begin revealing what it is that He wants you to do with your life and to lead you into the right decisions to fulfill His will.

CHAPTER IV
The Visits

It was time to start visiting the schools that Chad was possibly interested in attending. There were various issues that could affect his decision -- distance from home, his relationship with Katherine, academic programs and school reputation.

- What is the one consistent thing Chad does as he considers all of these options and issues?

- Read and Discuss Proverbs 3:5-6

As often is the case in the Christian life, the devil will try to find new ways to use old temptations. Chad is again tempted with sexual immorality.

- What circumstances would have made it easy for Chad to give into sexual temptation?

Chad was "furious" with the girl who claimed to be a Christian but saw nothing wrong with participating in sinful behavior.

- Read and Discuss James 1:22-25 and Romans 6:12-14
  Why should Christians refuse to sin even when they could "*get away with it*"?

PRAYER:
Ask God to remind you each day of the importance of prayer

CHAPTER V
Tragedy

Many people mistakenly believe that once you become a Christian everything in life should become easy. With the death of Jordan, Chad tragically discovered that very bad things can happen to good people.

Chad *"couldn't believe that God would let Jordan die."*

- What kind of tragedy have you experienced or witnessed that did not seem to "be fair"?

Chad came to the very important decision to turn this anger and doubt over to God and trust God.

- Read and Discuss Romans 8:28

- What might have happened to Chad's faith had he remained angry and doubtful?

Through this tragedy Chad came to a decision about the ultimate purpose for his life and all of his endeavors.

- What decision did Chad make?

- Read and Discuss I Corinthians 10:31

PRAYER
Share with God those things you have trouble accepting and understanding, and ask Him to strengthen your faith through them.

CHAPTER VI
The Season Begins

In the previous chapter Chad made the decision that he would live his life and play his game to the Glory of God. The season began and the competition was fierce. Derrick reminded Chad that even on the basketball court, his Christian faith could be challenged and had to be practiced.

- How important is it to realize that people are watching and evaluating your actions in light of your confessed faith?

- Read and Discuss Matthew 5:13-16

Chad quickly changed his attitude. Others may have called Chad a ***fanatic***, but he was trying to bring **all** of his life under the will of God.

- Read and Discuss Romans 12:1-2

There was one thing that Chad was deeply missing -- A close group of friends who shared his faith.

- Read and Discuss Hebrews 10:23-25

- Why is it important that we stay in fellowship with other Christians?

PRAYER
Ask God to show you areas of disobedience in your life, and ask for His help to bring these areas under submission to Him.

CHAPTER VII
New People At Church

In the last chapter we left Chad praying for new Christian friends. In Sunday School, Chad met Reece and Rachel. They seemed to be an answered prayer.

- Read and Discuss Matthew 7:7-12

- Do you believe God answers prayer? How have any of your prayers been answered?

Chad is very concerned that people who say they are Christian in fact behave like Christians. He observes them to decide how deeply they believe.

- Read and Discuss Matthew 7:15-20

- Do you feel that Chad is being judgmental or is he faithfully trying to discern a person's true beliefs?

Chad has found a girlfriend that shares his Christian values. He even makes his spiritual intentions clear to her in a very romantic way.

- If you had to come up with a list of rules/guidelines for Christian dating, what would some of them be?

PRAYER
Talk to God about a current relationship you are in, or ask God to lead you to the type of person He would want you to be with.

CHAPTER VIII
Katherine

It seems there was one person who was not happy for Chad and Rachel – Katherine.

- Why would Katherine act this way, even though she was the one who ended the relationship with Chad?

- Have you ever had anyone intent on making your life miserable?

Though Rachel was hurt by Katherine's attitude and Chad was very angered by her actions, the accident changed the picture entirely. They both ended up praying for Katherine.

- Read and Discuss Matthew 5:43-48

- What would make it difficult to pray for your enemies?

The scene in the hospital room clearly demonstrates the power of forgiveness. Rachel was especially forgiving and gracious.

- Read and Discuss Colossians 3:12-15

- Name a very dramatic time when Jesus forgave His enemies.

PRAYER
Who do you currently hold a grudge against, or who have you sinned against? Ask God to help you heal this relationship.

CHAPTER IX
The Record

Throughout his basketball career, people always counted on Chad to come through in a clutch, especially when the game was on the line. In the game against Jeffersonville, Chad came up short. He felt like he let everyone down.

- Read and Discuss Luke 22:31-34
  What did Peter end up doing?

- What are ways we might let Jesus down?

Chad came back the next game and finally broke the record. Rather than letting his failure in the previous game haunt him, he came back and played an exceptional game.

- Read and Discuss John 21:15-19
  What was Jesus telling Peter?

The Apostle Peter went on to be the leader of the early church. To do that he also had to forgive himself for his terrible failure.

- Why is it important to forgive yourself?

- What might make that hard to do?

PRAYER:
Confess your failures to Christ. Then ask for His forgiveness and ask for His help to forgive yourself.

CHAPTER X
The Sectional

The stakes are getting higher and higher for Chad and his team. Early in his Christian walk Chad made it a commitment and priority to keep God first, and that meant honoring God through his church attendance.

With an important game on the line and a special Wednesday practice called, Chad made the decision to keep church his first priority and was willing to sit out the game.

- Read and Discuss Joshua 24:5 and Matthew 6:24

- What do you think about Chad's decision?

- Was it right for his friends to react the way they did?

PRAYER

Make a list of the things you have been placing before God. Ask for God's forgiveness and promise God you will faithfully try to keep Him your first priority.

CHAPTER XI
The Semi State

With so much on the line you would think Derrick would have acted more wisely and with more consideration for others. His night of drinking jeopardized the chances for the whole team.

- Has anyone ever disappointed you greatly or let you down in an awful way?

Chad went out of his way to show Derrick understanding and compassion.
Others expressed their anger at Derrick.

- Read and Discuss James 5:19-20

- Did Chad point out Derrick's sin? Should he have?

- What do you think about the way Chad handled the situation with Derrick?

- What should we do when we see others sinning?

PRAYER
If you are concerned about the sin that a friend is committing, ask God for the wisdom you need to go to this friend and talk to them about their wrong actions.

CHAPTER XII
The State

Chad began a journey without Jesus Christ and ended his quest for a State Basketball Championship with Jesus Christ. As he looked back over the past years of his life, he saw that God had a wonderful hand in all of it.

- Read and Discuss Jeremiah 29:11

- What do you think about Chad publicly giving Jesus Christ all of the Glory in his speeches?

- In what ways can you speak up and give God glory in your life?

Earlier, in chapter five, you were asked to read and consider Romans 8:28.

- Up to this point, how have things, good and bad, worked together for the good in Chad's life?

Jordan had a very small part in this story, at the very beginning. And yet, everything that follows in the story has been influenced by his faithful desire to lead his friend to Christ.

- What does this story teach you about the importance of one person taking the time to lead a friend to Christ?

If someone were to write a quick summary of your life, perhaps an obituary, what would you like it to say?

PRAYER

Ask God to use you for His glory and to at least help make a special difference in another person's life.

About the Author:

Rusty W. Shepperd was born and raised in Indiana. Being raised in Indiana he was heavily influenced by his church, his family and, of course, basketball. First and foremost he is a Christian and would like this book to help Christian teens who may be struggling to lead a Christian life because of family, peers or just life in general. Lastly, Rusty would like to thank Jesus Christ, because without him none of the good things in his life would have happened, and Jon Lineback for all the help he provided during his endeavor to get this book published.

Made in the USA
Lexington, KY
23 March 2010